ORGANIC
EMBROIDERY

Meredith Woolnough

Other Schiffer Books on Related Subjects:

Artistry in Fiber, Vol. 1: Wall Art, Anne Lee, E. Ashley Rooney, Foreword by Marcia Young, Introduction by Meredith Re' Grimsley, ISBN 978-0-7643-5304-8

Artistry in Fiber, Vol. 2: Sculpture, Anne Lee, E. Ashley Rooney, Foreword by Lois Russell, Introduction by Adrienne Sloane, ISBN 978-0-7643-5342-0

Artistry in Fiber, Vol. 3: Wearable Art, Anne Lee, E. Ashley Rooney, Foreword by Susan Taber Avila, Foreword by Margery Goldberg, ISBN 978-0-7643-5399-4

Designed by Insight Design Concepts ltd.

Type set in Bauer Bodoni and Bliss
ISBN: 978-0-7643-5613-1
Printed in China

Published by Schiffer Publishing, Ltd.
4880 Lower Valley Road
Atglen, PA 19310
Phone: (610) 593-1777; Fax: (610) 593-2002
E-mail: Info@schifferbooks.com
Web: www.schifferbooks.com

For our complete selection of fine books on this and related subjects, please visit our website at www.schifferbooks.com. You may also write for a free catalog.

Schiffer Publishing's titles are available at special discounts for bulk purchases for sales promotions or premiums. Special editions, including personalized covers, corporate imprints, and excerpts, can be created in large quantities for special needs. For more information, contact the publisher.

We are always looking for people to write books on new and related subjects. If you have an idea for a book, please contact us at proposals@schifferbooks.com.

Note
Artwork sizes are all framed sizes unless specified.

ORGANIC
EMBROIDERY

Meredith Woolnough

4880 Lower Valley Road • Atglen, PA 19310

CONTENTS

Research and Development

Fieldwork	13
Drawing	34
Color Matching	38
Field Photography	44
Collecting Specimens	52
Further Research	60
Developing Artwork Designs for Embroidery	72

Introduction

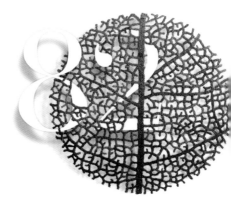

Drawing with a Sewing Machine

Tools and Materials	86
Getting Started	90
Single-Line Stitching	92
Dense Stitching	98
Zigzag Stitching	105
Thinking in Layers	110
Color Blending	112

Dissolving and Sculpting

The Dissolving Process   122

Basic Dissolving   124

Supported Dissolving   133

Molding and Sculpting   136

Designing for Three Dimensions   140

Tips and Troubleshooting

Tips, Tricks, and Trade Secrets   148

Sewing Machine Setup Tips   151

Machine Maintenance   158

Drawing on Water-Soluble Fabric   160

Stitching Tips   164

Dissolving Tips   172

Quick Troubleshooting Guide   175

References and Acknowledgments

Introduction

There is so much wonder and beauty in the world around us if we choose to take the time to look. My art-making journey is all about exploring and reimagining the natural world through embroidery, and I hope that I can inspire you to do the same.

For more than ten years I have been making art using a unique embroidery technique. This simple way of stitching is highly versatile and allows me to transform a domestic sewing machine into an unconventional drawing tool. By using a base fabric that washes away in water, I can create stitched drawings that transform from two-dimensional embroideries into three-dimensional sculptures.

I first discovered this way of working during my fine art studies at university. Captivated by the creative and sculptural possibilities of this technique, I spent an entire year experimenting and playing with ways to draw and sculpt with thread. In that year I made lots of mistakes, but I also learned so much about this wonderful process and its raw potential for art making. Since then I have continued to hone and perfect my craft, evolving those early experiments into my current nature-inspired artworks.

This book will take you on a tour through my art practice, acting as an instructional guide for those who seek to learn these techniques and use them in their own art making. As you explore this book you will follow my creative process; from the initial fieldwork and research that influences my designs through to the technical production of my embroidered artworks.

Scattered throughout the book you will find examples of my embroidery. In these artwork features you can read the stories behind each piece and learn about the fascinating natural subjects that inspired me to create them.

My aim for this book is to provide an instructional and inspirational resource tool suitable for all levels of creators and makers. I hope that my practice will motivate you to get outdoors more, to experience nature, and to use its wonders to inspire your own original artworks. I hope that you can learn from my experiences, and I wish you great success with your own stitched creations.

Happy sewing.
Meredith

Research and Development

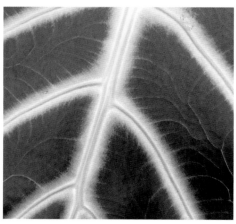

My creative process starts with fieldwork. This is where I draw, photograph, and study the natural specimens that I encounter. Fieldwork allows me to produce my own visual resources to inspire and inform my work. Further research and scientific identification of my finds help to build up a solid understanding of my subjects. I believe that these practices create more accurate and original artworks.

Fieldwork

Whenever I need inspiration for a new artwork I go out into the natural environment. Being out in nature is always a very spiritual experience for me; it is humbling to consider the larger world and my place within it. Aside from being a very pleasurable activity, fieldwork is a type of practice-based research that provides real opportunities to collect primary resources to inspire and inform artworks.

Fieldwork doesn't have to be difficult or even purposeful. A simple walk around your garden or local area may provide all that you need to get the creative juices flowing. Always be on the watch for interesting things when you are out and about: you never know what may be just under your nose. That pretty leaf you incidentally picked up on a walk to the mailbox could be the start of a wonderful artwork.

Incidental fieldwork is great, but there may be times when a more planned expedition is necessary. You might be seeking a specific plant or animal to study, or you may be visiting a unique area that you want to record. Whatever your reason for doing fieldwork, it is good practice to be well prepared so you know what you might find and how best to record it if you do. When I conduct fieldwork I try to pack light: everything I take has to fit inside a backpack or it doesn't come with me.

My fieldwork equipment
- Camera
- Sketchbook
- My fieldwork drawing kit
- Bottle of water (to drink and for watercolor painting)
- Field guides suitable to my location and area of interest

My fieldwork drawing kit is a small fishing-tackle box. This box has many little adjustable compartments so I can make all of my equipment fit snugly. The kit houses some basic drawing equipment (pencils, pens, and erasers), a travel watercolor set, brushes, and a few other tools (scissors, tissues, and zip-lock bags for specimen collection).

For me, fieldwork is all about observing, recording, and visually interpreting the natural world. When I find something that catches my attention in the field, I will first spend some time simply looking at it, trying to take it all in and understand it. I will then record my observations in a sketchbook with drawings and notes. Photographs are taken from various angles and, if permitted, I will collect some specimens so that I can study them in closer detail once back in the comfort of my studio.

Scribbly Gum Leaf

I can't walk past a fascinating leaf! Whenever I see a leaf that has an interesting shape or is a striking color I will collect it. My sketchbooks and pockets end up full of them.

Gum tree leaves are the leaves that I seem to collect the most. I have always loved how these otherwise very straight, slender leaves can curl up on themselves when they dry, forming spiraled shapes. On one occasion I found a leaf that had curled up into an almost perfect circle. This curious leaf inspired my large wall mounted artwork called *Scribbly Gum Leaf.*

To develop this artwork I photographed the leaf specimen, printed the photo, and painstakingly traced out each individual vein. This drawing was then enlarged to more than three feet (one meter) in diameter to act as a template for the embroidery.

This is the largest singular embroidered artwork that I have created to date and, unsurprisingly, it took me several months to stitch.

Kingdom: Plantae
Family: Myrtaceae
Genus: *Eucalyptus*
Species: *E. haemastoma*

Scribbly Gum Leaf (*Eucalyptus haemastoma*),
2014, polyester thread, 3 feet (1 meter) diameter.

Botanical fieldwork

Botanical fieldwork can be practiced anywhere that plants grow. Local environments and private gardens are great places to start, because not only are they accessible, they also provide the opportunity to observe and record seasonal changes over subsequent visits. National parks are another great place to conduct fieldwork because they provide plants growing unconstrained in their natural habitats, free from human intervention and cultivation.

Botanical gardens are also one of my favorite places to study plants. They are great sources of artistic inspiration and beautiful places to visit. Botanical gardens display a wide variety of native and exotic plants within a contained and controlled area. Generally, the plants are in great health so you are seeing a specimen at its best. Most plants come with convenient name tags that will kick-start your research by aiding identification.

Botanical drawing and annotation

When choosing a plant to study, pick a specimen that displays a lot of information. Rather than just selecting a single leaf, focus on the larger plant so that you can describe all of its elements and features. Start by describing the overall shape and size of the plant. Then focus on the individual elements that interest you, such as leaves, bark, seeds, fruit, and flowers. Record the shape, texture, and color of each part of the plant, paying special attention to how these elements connect. Aim to draw your specimen to scale. If this isn't possible you can record the scale in your notes or photograph the specimen next to something of a known size.

As you sketch you can write little notes alongside your drawing. These annotations describe elements that may not be clear or that you haven't managed to capture in your drawing. Elements such as texture or color can be difficult to describe in a quick sketch, so a written note can instead record this information. Don't feel that you have to make your notes highly scientific or use technical botanical terminology—your notes just need to be descriptive and make sense to you.

Fieldwork at the Hunter Region Botanic Gardens,
Port Stephens, NSW, Australia.

Fieldwork - Hunter region
Botanic gardens : Thursday 5th
Pond (near the front of the gardens)
Sunny day/some occasional cloudcover

WATER LILIES
(Nymphaeaceae)

Flower:
· vivid fuscia colour
· centre - yellow.
· petals radiating out
of centre (unfolding)
· Flowers close at
night
→ indicate that these
are day blooming tropical
lilies - Brachyceras?

Round
Shape
(orbicular)

Field sk

other colours in the pond:
· blue
· white   · pink
· yellow   · orange
· yellow-peach-pink

Leaves
· Top surface is smooth
& 'waxy' with a shine
· Leaf venation is more
defined on the underside
of the leaf
· leaves float on the
surface or
lie (reig
abg

Stem from
centre of leaf

Radial not

Botanical fieldwork cheat sheet

Environment:
- Date/time/weather
- Location
- Habitat type
- Where you found your plant

Identification:
- Common name
- Scientific name

Leaves:
- Size and shape
- The tip and base of the leaf
- The leaf margins
- Vein pattern
- Leaf arrangement
- Texture
- Color

Flowers:
- Size and shape
- Symmetry of the flower
- Petal shape, number of petals, and their arrangement
- Texture
- Center of the flower (male and female organs)
- Buds/young flowers
- Dead and dying flowers (what is left behind)
- How the flower is connected to the rest of the plant
- Color

Fruit/Seeds/Nuts
- Size and shape
- Internal structure
- Arrangement
- Color
- Surface texture
- Seed pods

Other Notable Features:
- Bark
- Stems
- Roots
- Thorns, spines, and prickles
- Tendrils
- Scent
- Damage
- Behavior
- Surrounding plants and animals

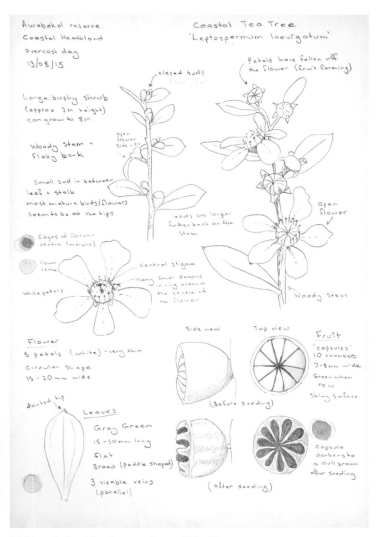

Awabakal reserve.
Coastal Heathland
overcast day
13/08/15

Coastal Tea Tree
'Leptospermum laevigatum'

Large bushy shrub
(approx 3m height)
can grow to 8m.

Woody Stem +
Flaky bark

Small bud in between
leaf + stalk
most mature buds/flowers
seem to be at the tips

closed buds

Petals have fallen off
the flower (fruit forming)

open
flower
side view

Open
flower

leaves are larger
further back on the
stem

Woody Stem

Edges of flower
centre (maroon)

flower
centre

white petals

central stigma

Many small stamens
in ring around
the centre of
the flower

Flower
5 petals (white) - very thin
Circular shape
15 - 20 mm wide

Pointed tip

Leaves
Grey Green
15 - 30 mm long
Flat
Broad (paddle shaped)
3 visable veins
(parallel)

Side view

Top view

(Before Seeding)

(after seeding)

Fruit
'capsules'
10 chambers
7 - 8 mm wide
Green when
new
Shiny surface.

capsule
darkens to
a dull brown
after seeding

11/03/17
Don Morris Walk
By the river / rainforest
Hot / sunny day / Humid

common: Slender Grape
scientific: Cayratia clematidea

Soft flexible stem

Stem cross
section is square

Leaf colour
deep/vibrant green

Vein colour
(lighter & more yellow)

Vine grows vertically
Branching out to 'catch'
new veins & trees to anchor to
Not growing above 1 meter

Tendril
Grows out on
the opposite side
of leaflets.

Leaves -
• Ovulate
• Serrated margin
• Pinnate
venation

• 5 leaflets
one larger one (central)
Two pairs on either side sharing
the same stem.

'Herbaceous scrambler'
• flowers/seeds/fruit not present/
unknown

leaves hanging downward
Drooping Slightly *

* This specimen was in full sun
at the time of drawing - they
may be drooping due to
dehydration.

* Clippings taken droop &
dehydrate quickly. They
need to be drawn/photographed
within half an hour of collection

pointed
tip

The slender grape
was growing up
another woody
vine (species unknown)

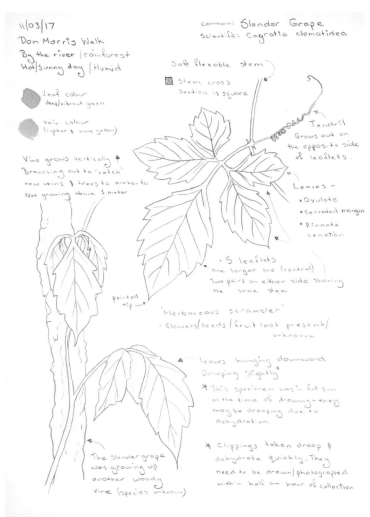

Fieldwork sketchbook page, Coastal Tea Tree

(Leptospermum laevigatum)

Fieldwork sketchbook page, Slender Grape

(Cayratia clematidea)

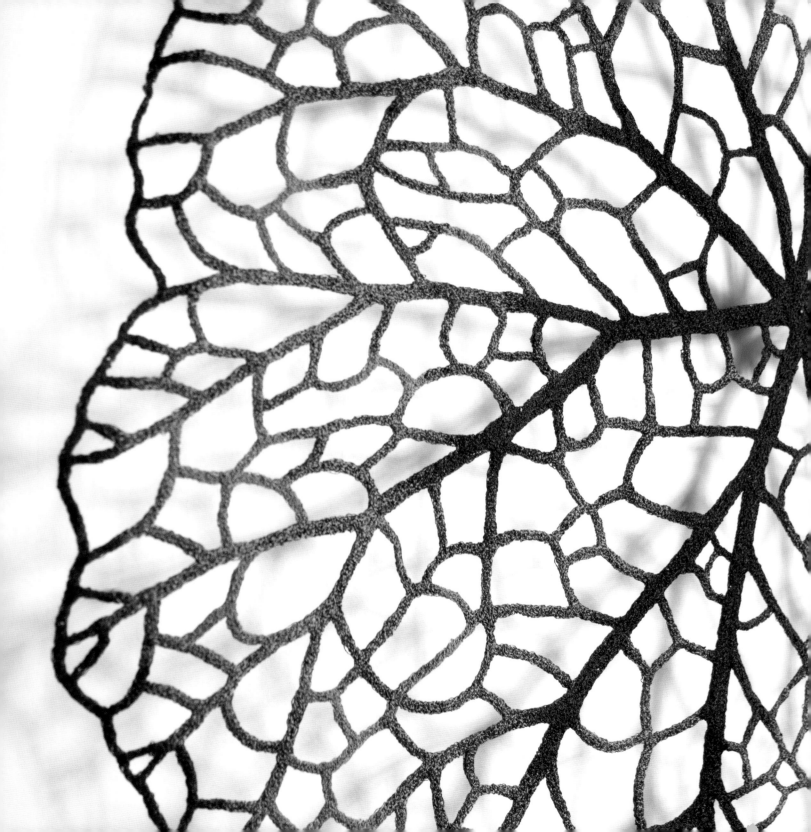

Begonia Leaves

Begonia Leaf # 1 and # 2 were inspired by a serendipitous visit to the Ballarat Botanical Gardens during its annual begonia festival. I was teaching a workshop in the area and came across the event while exploring the gardens on my afternoon off.

The festival showcases a huge collection of begonia varieties in the main greenhouse. The many vibrant flowers made the whole display explode with color, but it was the leaves that I was most drawn to. There is huge variety in the shape, patterning, and color of begonia leaves. I personally love the asymmetrical leaf varieties with bands of purple and green.

Kingdom: Plantae
Order: Cucurbitales
Family: Begoniaceae
Genus: *Begonia*

Display of begonias at the Ballarat Botanical Gardens showing some of their variety of decorative leaf shapes and color.

Begonia Leaf #1, *2016, polyester thread and pins on paper, 32 x 26in (82 x 66cm).*

Begonia Leaf #2, *2016, polyester thread and pins on paper, 32 x 26in (82 x 66cm).*

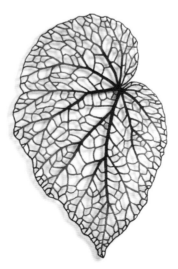
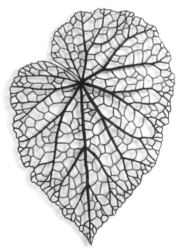

Marine fieldwork

I love the ocean. It is like an alien world full of weird and wonderful things. There is so much inspiration to be found just beneath the surface. I explore the ocean and its surrounds whenever possible. Marine fieldwork is my favorite type of fieldwork.

Fieldwork on the beach

The beach is a great place for fieldwork because lots of interesting things wash up on the shore. I always find plenty of interesting shells, algae, and hydroid specimens for study at my local beach.

Rock pools are also interesting ecosystems to study, with many plants and animals coexisting in one small environment. If you are planning to do fieldwork in rock pools, time your visit with a very low tide so you can access the pools safely.

Shells inspire several of my artworks and I have a vast collection of them in my studio. When studying shells pay attention to their overall shape, color, surface texture, patterning, and any ridges, bumps, or ribs. All of these features can help aid identification. I like to draw shells from various angles to get a clear understanding of their form.

Underwater fieldwork

I do a lot of snorkeling and scuba diving to collect primary material to inspire my marine-based works. This type of fieldwork is a lot of fun, but it does present some unique challenges.

*Red coralline algae (*Amphiroa beauvoisii*) specimen found washed up on the beach.*

Sketchbook shell studies.

It is difficult to draw underwater. Even with an underwater slate it is very challenging to draw well when bobbing around in the ocean. I tend to get lost in my drawing when I am underwater and spend all of my precious dive time looking at my slate rather than at the beautiful marine wonderland around me. Now I don't bother with underwater sketching anymore. Instead, I spend my time observing and taking photographs.

I find that the most powerful tool for working underwater is simple observation. The more we look the more we learn. By simply taking the time to observe something closely we can develop a deep understanding and appreciation of it. I spend a lot of time just looking at coral while diving or snorkeling and this observation builds up a visual library in my mind that I can later recall when developing a coral-based design.

The photographs I take underwater become another valuable reference when I am developing artwork designs. I only have a very basic underwater camera and as a result my photos are murky and dark. Despite this, they capture all of the information I need.

Coral reefs are my favorite natural environments to explore. These are beautiful and very busy places, with so much to see. Many of my artworks are inspired by coral because I am fascinated by these animals and the amazing structures they build.

If you are studying coral make sure you get up close and examine the individual corallites. These are the small skeletal cups that house the coral polyps. Coral identification is largely determined by their size and arrangement.

Snorkeling is a fun, easy way to explore the water.

Scuba diving is a wonderful way to fully immerse yourself in the underwater world.

Free diving is a great way to explore shallow marine environments.

Red Coral

My love for coral has stemmed from experiences scuba diving. I first learned to dive while on the Great Barrier Reef back in 2004, and have been seeking out the world's best coral reefs ever since.

The red coral series consists of a range of branching coral forms depicted in vivid red thread. The series began as a comment on the issue of red coral harvesting for use in jewelry and the very questionable sustainability of the practice. It has since evolved into a study of the many coral species that have this brilliant coloring.

My coral pieces are presented like delicate organic specimens, carefully pinned to the wall, available for close inspection and study. My coral artworks are a guilt-free piece of the ocean that people can proudly display in their homes, showing the beauty and intricacies of coral colonies without the need to rip coral from its natural habitat.

Giant Sea Fan, 2013, polyester thread and pins on paper, 43 x 37in (110 x 93cm). It is one of the largest red coral pieces I have created to date.

Gorgonian fans (or Alcyonacea) are one of my favorites things to see on a dive. These beautiful lacelike structures can grow to enormous sizes and come in a huge variety of vibrant colors.

Kingdom: Animalia
Phylum: Cnidaria
Class: Anthozoa
Subclass: Octocorallia
Order: Alcyonacea

Coral Branch, 2012, polyester thread and pins on paper, 20 x 26in (50 x 65cm).

1

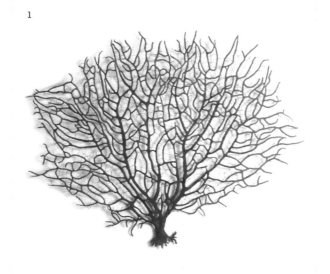

2

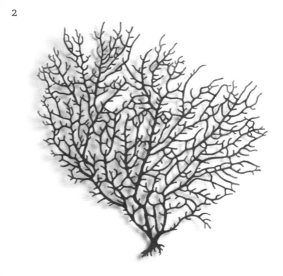

3

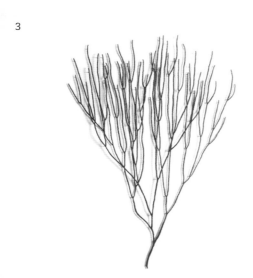

4

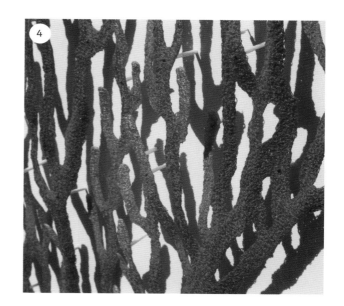

1. Red Coral Fan, *2016, polyester thread and pins on paper, 33 x 29in (85 x 73cm).*

2. Red Coral (*Corallium rebrum*), *2016, 29 x 29in (73 x 73cm).*

3. Sea Whip, *2017, polyester thread and pins on paper, 43 x 33in (110 x 85cm).*

4. Giant Coral Branch *detail.*

This piece is based on the sea fan, *Ctenocella pectinata*. This harp (lyre) or comb-shaped sea fan grows in two distinct branches with many thin, long branchlets arising from the topside of its branches. These fans can grow to large sizes (almost 5ft/150cm) wide and are generally a vibrant red color.

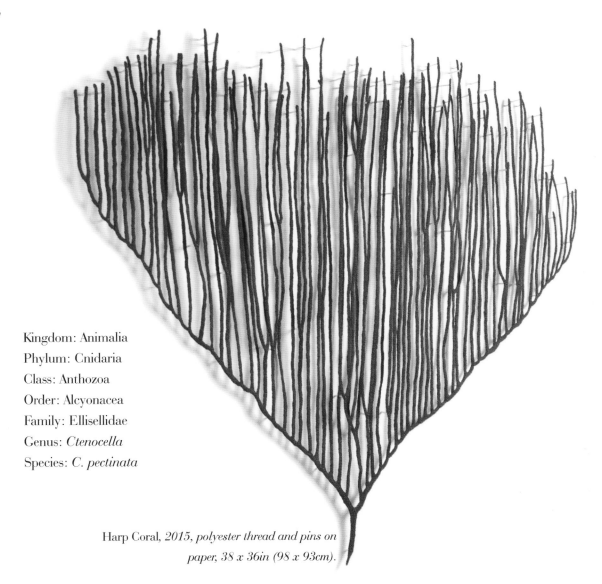

Kingdom: Animalia
Phylum: Cnidaria
Class: Anthozoa
Order: Alcyonacea
Family: Ellisellidae
Genus: *Ctenocella*
Species: *C. pectinata*

Harp Coral, *2015, polyester thread and pins on paper, 38 x 36in (98 x 93cm).*

29

Fieldwork in aquariums

Aquariums are great places to do marine fieldwork. They are especially good if you can't get access to the ocean or you don't want to get wet. In aquariums you will find many aquatic flora and fauna all in one place. You always know that a particular species will be there on any given day and you can revisit if necessary. Aquariums allow you to get up really close to marine life and draw and photograph them without the challenges of underwater fieldwork. I often get much better photographs from outside the tank than I could ever capture underwater.

The best thing about doing fieldwork in aquariums is that there are expert staff nearby that can help you with identification and any other questions you may have about an exhibit. Consulting with experts is a fantastic way to research and to learn new things.

Photographing animals in captivity needs to be done with sensitivity and patience. Always avoid using flash, especially with animals in low light conditions because it will scare, and maybe even harm, them.

Below: I rarely see Discosoma *(mushroom coral) in the wild but they are common inhabitants in aquariums.* Discosoma, *in particular this red variety, have inspired many of my artworks and installations including* The New Neighbours *(108).*

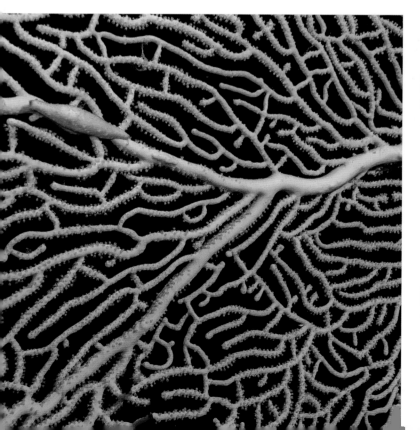

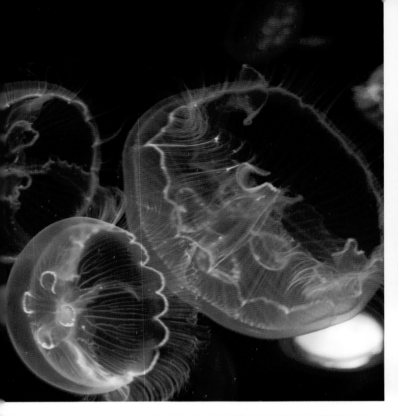

Left: I have never seen a nautilus in the wild because they live at great depths, but I am fascinated by these prehistoric cephalopods and I am always very excited if they are a part of an aquarium's collection. Nautilus are difficult to photograph even in aquariums because they are kept in very dark tanks that mimic their natural environment. For this shot I was lucky enough to have this nautilus come up close to the glass and allow me to take a few quick shots before it disappeared back into the gloom of the tank.

Fan Worm Crown

An ocean creature that has always fascinated and delighted me on dives is the fan worm, *Sabella spallanzanii*. This little annelid is otherwise known as the European fan worm, pencil worm, or feather duster worm, and is found in shallow, sub-tidal areas. If you wave your hand close to a fan worm it will instantly pull its feathery feeding tentacles back inside its tube. They move surprisingly fast for an animal that is permanently embedded in the reef. Fan worms can be tricky to photograph in the ocean but I was able to get some decent shots of this species in an aquarium.

My *Fan Worm Crown* artwork focuses on the worm's crown of feeding tentacles, of which there are two distinct layers. However it is difficult to see this layered structure when the tentacles are extended in the water, as they mostly just look like a soft cup or feathery plume waving in the current. If you were to take the tentacles out of the water and flatten them out you would see the structure that has inspired my artwork. I hoped to show the beauty and complexity of the worm's crown in this piece, highlighting its mathematical perfection and delicate color banding.

Kingdom: Animalia
Phylum: Annelida
Class: Polychaeta
Order: Sabellida
Family: Sabellidae
Genus: *Sabella*
Species: *S. spallanzanii*

Fan Worm Crown
(*Sabella spallanzanii*), *2016,*
polyester thread and pins on paper,
37 x 37in (93 x 93cm).

Drawing

Drawing something is always better than simply taking a photo of it. Drawing forces you to focus, slow down, and think deeply about what you are looking at. This intense, direct observation helps to develop a clearer understanding of your subject. Through the act of drawing, you will often pick up on many vital elements that may otherwise be overlooked.

I have always seen drawing as a vital part of my practice, particularly as a tool to better understand my subjects. Through my drawing I feel that I develop a better connection with the subject and this becomes crucial when developing designs for my embroideries. When preparing for a new artwork I will draw the same subject many times: this helps to develop a familiarity and deep understanding about the subject.

Drawing in the field

Field drawings don't have to be an exact likeness. They are simply a way to capture information quickly and describe what you have found. A few pencil lines describing the basic shape, form, and structure of your subject is all you need. A sketch will be faster, and often more effective at describing your subject than a written description will ever be. If you are describing a complex form, try drawing your subject from various angles to build up a complete picture of it.

My field sketches are quickly done and often very messy. If there are elements that my drawing didn't manage to capture, such as the texture or scent, I will make a little written note of this next to the drawing. My sketches and annotations work together to build up the picture of what I am describing.

Drawing basics

Many people lack confidence when it comes to drawing, simply stating that they "can't draw." I believe that anyone can draw well if they put their mind to it and consistently work at refining their skills. Drawing is largely a learned skill and accurate drawing comes with practice and perseverance. Don't be afraid of drawing, even if you think your drawing skills are lacking. Just give it a go. You may be surprised at what you produce and how much pleasure you get from the process.

The secret to good drawing is to really look at your subject; study it. The more you look, the more you see. The more you see, the more accurate your drawings will be. There are many different ways to approach a drawing and no one way is necessarily better than any other.

When I draw, I start by plotting out the overall shape of my subject with some basic line work. I then refine the drawing by correcting misplaced lines and adding details until I feel I have captured my subject well. The more you draw the easier and quicker the process will become.

Maidenhair fieldwork sketchbook page

One way to draw a leaf

If you lack confidence when it comes to drawing, my advice is to start simple. A line drawing of a flat leaf is a great subject to start with because you only need to worry about capturing its basic shape and structure. Below I have outlined one way you can approach drawing leaves. This same drawing approach can then be applied to almost anything.

Find a leaf that interests you. Before you start to draw, spend a few minutes simply looking at your leaf. Analyze all the details, textures, tones, and colors before you put pencil to paper. We often expect things in nature to be perfectly symmetrical, but this is rarely the case. Look for the asymmetry in your subjects: the differences and the imperfections. It is these little things that you notice and capture that will make your drawings more accurate and help you to build a deeper connection with your subject.

Visualize how you are going to construct the drawing and plan how it will fit onto your page. Draw the stem and mid-vein—this will usually be one continuous line. Then draw the leaf blade around the central vein. Fill in the more prominent secondary veins. Pay attention to the number of veins, their position, and whether or not they curve and fork within the leaf. Continue to refine the drawing to show any special characteristics of the leaf—perhaps a serrated edge or a rounded tip.

Maple leaf: This Japanese maple leaf is drawn using the same process; the only difference is that the mid-veins of each leaflet are included in the first step.

Color Matching

Color is vitally important in any artwork and it is often the element that people are first drawn to. I make a point of noting the original colors of the specimens that I am studying, and then refer back to these when developing a color scheme for an artwork.

Many natural specimens, especially plants, will change color over time. For this reason it is important to take note of the original colors and tones of your nature finds so you have a record for future reference. I like to use watercolor paints to make small color swatches when I do my fieldwork.

Watercolor is a great medium for fieldwork and sketchbook painting because it is a quick, relatively mess free way to add accurate color to a drawing. I work with a small travel set of watercolor paints. This set is very easy to work with in the field; I only need a brush and a bit of water to get painting. My watercolor set is a mix of warm and cool primary colors (reds, blues, and yellows). With these colors I can mix up any hue I desire to make accurate color swatches.

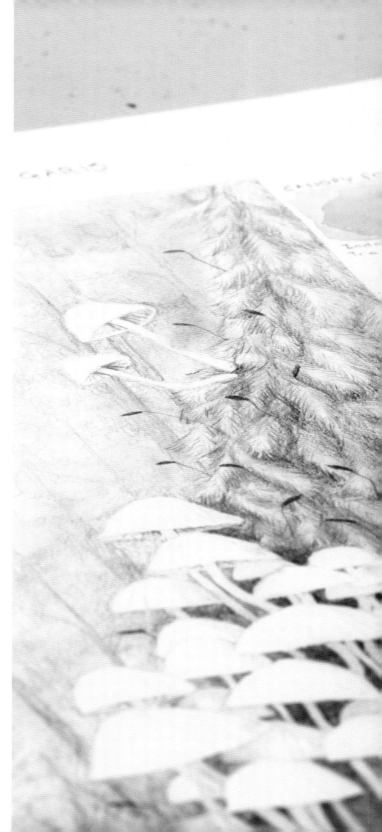

This graphite drawing depicts the fungi species Mycena vulgaris *in its rainforest habitat. The drawing includes a number of watercolor swatches in the borders of the drawing, indicating the range of browns and greens found in the habitat.*

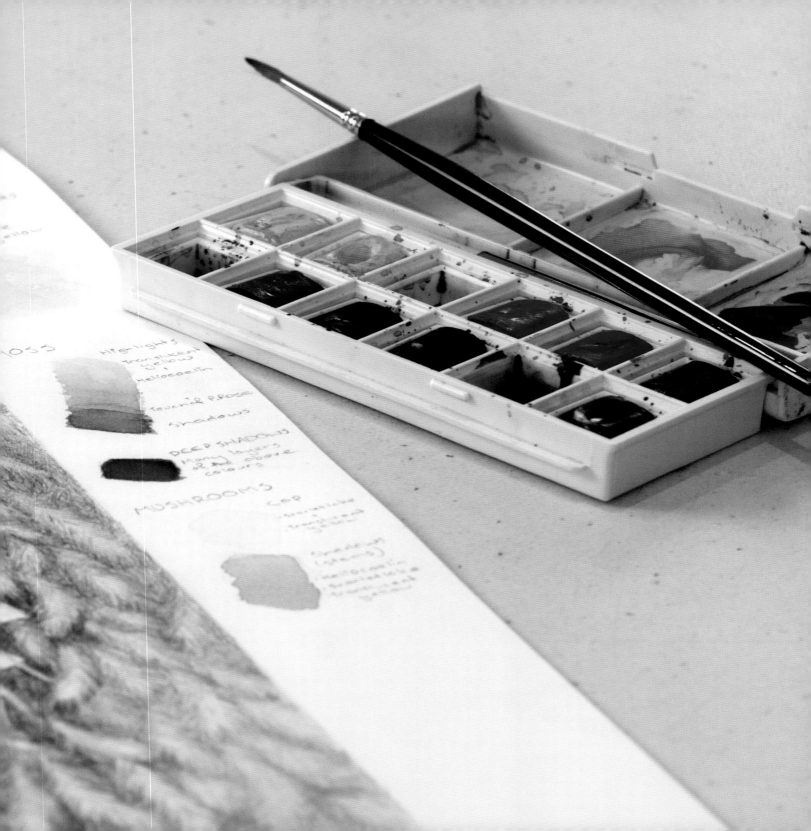

Watercolor studies of found eucalyptus leaves.

This fieldwork sketchbook page describes a gristle fern (Blechum cartilagineum) *leaf. The notes include initial color-matching swatches and a pressed plant specimen that has subsequently darkened and lost its color as it dried.*

Leaf Wreath, *2014,*
watercolor on paper. After
an especially good leaf haul
I was inspired to paint this
little wreath painting in
watercolors.

Maple Seed

I have always loved the distinctive seeds of the maple tree. These seeds are properly called "samaras," but more playfully known as "helicopters," "whirly birds," or simply "maple keys." These seedpods are iconic because of their unique shape and the way they twirl and spin as they fall from the tree. When the seeds are young they are a vivid green color that fades to a soft pink at the tip of the wing. I remember playing with many maple seeds as a child, imagining that they were fairy wings.

My *Maple Seed* is inspired by the beautiful shape and coloring of young samaras. Working from a dried specimen, I carefully mapped the intricate veining network on the outer surface of the seed. I then stitched the design in the vivid greens and pinks I remember from my youth. In this instance, I used a range of photographs to inform my color matching as I only had access to dried, brown specimens.

Kingdom: Plantae
Clade: Angiosperms
Order: Sapindales
Family: Sapindaceae
Genus: *Acer*
Species: *A. palmatum*

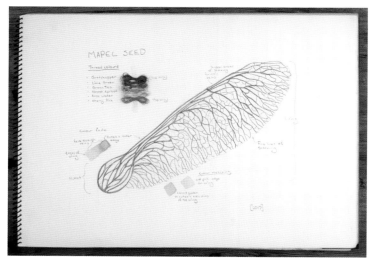

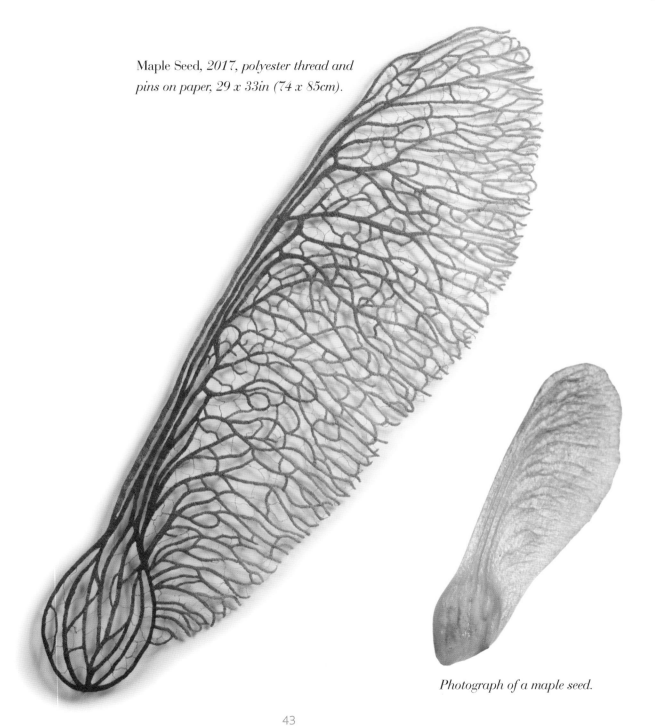

Maple Seed, *2017, polyester thread and pins on paper, 29 x 33in (74 x 85cm).*

Photograph of a maple seed.

Field Photography

Field photography is a great way to collect original visual resources to inspire and inform artworks. This type of photography is not about taking a beautiful photograph: its goal is to capture the details and features of what you have found in the field, so that your nature find can be identified and studied.

You don't need fancy equipment for field photography. A basic point-and-shoot camera or the camera on a cell phone will suffice. A digital SLR camera with a range of lenses will provide greater control over the images you collect, but it is not necessary.

Field photography involves taking several photos to build up the full story of the specimen. If you approach field photography in a systematic way, with a clear idea of the types of photographs you need to collect, you won't miss anything. Below is a suggested shoot list for studying flowering plants in the field. By following this list you will develop a good library of photographs that describe the various elements of the plant. This will aid identification and future study. Not all of the listed elements will be present on a plant at one time: fruit, flowers, and seeds occur at different times so you may require repeat visits to capture these elements.

Shoot list for a flowering plant

- **Habitat** an overall shot that describes the shape and size of the plant. It may also describe how and where it grows and its relationship with any neighboring elements.
- **Individual branch** showing the leaves and any other elements that are present (flowers, fruit, seeds, etc.). Make sure you can see how these elements attach to the branch.
- **Individual leaf** shoot both the top and underside of the leaf.
- **Flowers** front, top, and side views.
- **Seeds and seedpods** including open seedpods to show individual seeds if possible.
- **Fruit**
- **Bark**
- **Any other interesting features**

If you collect cut specimens for study it is a good practice to shoot these individually, on a plain background alongside something that shows scale. I find that a blank page of my sketchbook works well for a background and I carry a small ruler in my drawing kit for scale.

Flowering plant field photography
example: Water lilies.

1. Habitat.
2. Closer habitat with flower bud.
3. Flower—side view.
4. Flower—top view.
5. Detail of flower center.
6. Underside of leaf.
7. Leaf—top view.
8. Collected specimens with ruler for scale.

I have created several artworks inspired by lily pads. I am particularly drawn to the strong vein patterning and vibrant colors on the underside of the leaves. So the first thing I do when I encounter a lily pond is flip a few leaves over. Water lily specimens lose their vibrant color and distort when they dry out, so it is important to photograph the specimens when they are fresh to get an accurate record to work from.

One of my favorite subjects to photograph during botanical fieldwork is an illuminated leaf. To do this, simply hold an individual leaf up to the sun so that it is backlit. This will highlight the vein structures within the leaf.

I love the great variety in leaf veins and can't go past an interesting leaf without zooming in on its vein structure. This is one of the reasons that I love to do my own fieldwork. I get to look at things in great detail and see the tiny elements that many others miss.

Leaf veins provide support for the leaf and transport water and food for the plant. Although they all do the same basic job, there is so much variety in how the veins curve and network within the leaf.

Underwater field photography

Underwater photography can be a lot of fun but it is also challenging. There are several things that should be taken into consideration:

- Colors change with depth; the deeper you go the less color you will see. As a result, underwater photographs are rarely accurate resources for color-matching unless you have supplementary lighting.
- Underwater animals are often fast-moving and can be difficult to photograph, especially since we are so slow underwater. Be patient when photographing animals and never chase or provoke them. Just photograph what you can.
- Sedentary specimens—such as corals and algae—can be photographed in a more systematic way. Try to capture different angles and details in your photographs, so that later you have lots of reference material to work from.

I use a GoPro for underwater photography. This camera does not provide any supplementary lighting, and as a result my underwater shots are often blurry and very blue-toned. While my underwater fieldwork photos won't win any photography prizes, they provide ample information to aid identification and inspire my creativity.

Recording three-dimensional objects

When photographing or drawing three-dimensional objects it is good practice to record multiple views of your specimen. This will give you a good idea of its form and overall structure. Wherever possible collect a front, side, and top view as a minimum. You may find that you need multiple side views if the form is as complex as this shell.

This murex shell has a complex form that is difficult to describe in a single photograph. To build up a complete record of its form the shell has been photographed several times, at differing angles.

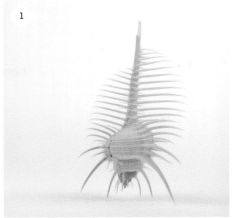

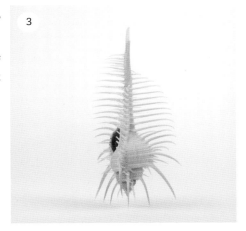

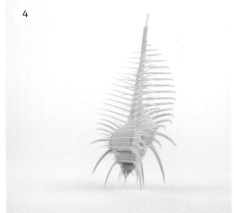

1. *Murex shell, side view 1.*
2. *Murex shell, side view 2.*
3. *Murex shell, side view 3.*
4. *Murex shell, side view 4.*
5. *Murex shell, top view.*
6. *Murex shell, view of underside.*

Spirula spirula

I love to collect and photograph the things that appear on my local beach. This photograph was taken at sunrise, capturing a tiny spiraled shell I had found. These shells have always intrigued me. They wash up on the beach in great numbers but only a few times a year. Measuring about 1 inch wide, these shells are bone white and surprisingly strong for such a light, delicate structure. I always assumed that these shells were broken segments of a much larger spiral shell and I was forever on the hunt for a "complete specimen" to study. After some research I discovered that these shells were originally the internal calcified shell of a deep-sea squid called *Spirula spirula*.

Spirula is one of the few cephalopods in existence that still retains a shell. The spirally coiled shell is composed of a series of chambers that provide buoyancy control for the squid. A small thread-like tube, called a siphuncle, runs through these chambers and the *Spirula* can regulate its density (and therefore buoyancy) by transporting gases and fluid between these chambers via the tube. Only cephalopods with chambered shells have siphuncles, making them quite a unique shell adaptation.

In my embroidered artwork *Spirula spirula* I wanted to depict the shell as if it had been cut in half, exposing the various chambers and the siphuncle that runs through the shell.

Kingdom: Animalia
Phylum: Mollusca
Class: Cephalopoda
Order: Spirulida
Family: Spirulidae
Genus: *Spirula*
Species: *S. spirula*

1. *Scientific illustration of a* Spirula spirula
   squid and shell. Ink on paper, 2016.
2. Spirula spirula shell, *2017, polyester thread
   and pins on paper, 20 x 27in (53 x 69cm).*
3. Spirula spirula shell—*angled view.*
4. Spirula spirula shell—*detail.*

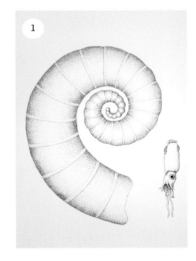

Collecting Specimens

Nothing beats having and holding the real thing when it comes to studying an element from nature. I find that when I work from a real-life specimen my drawings are clearer and more accurate, my color notation is spot on, and I feel a much deeper connection with my subject. That is what makes specimen collection such a valuable tool for inspiring artworks and it is why I like to work from life wherever possible.

Specimen collection doesn't need to be complicated. Most nature lovers will already be in the habit of picking up interesting things that they find while out in nature. I have always collected bits and pieces from that natural world—my pockets are invariably lined with interesting shells, rocks, seedpods, and fallen leaves that I have picked up when I am out and about. However, while it is fine to collect fallen leaves and abandoned shells, some natural specimens should never be collected.

Living animals should never be removed from their natural environments and you may need permission to collect certain plant specimens. Whenever you plan to collect specimens, investigate the area and check if specimen collection is permitted. In certain areas (national parks, protected areas, marine sanctuaries, etc.) you are not permitted to collect specimens without prior written permission from the governing body of that area. In many cases you are not permitted to take specimens at all. If you are not sure if an area is protected or where to go to gain permission for collection, do not collect specimens from that area. No matter how tempting they are. Your photographs and field sketches will have to be enough.

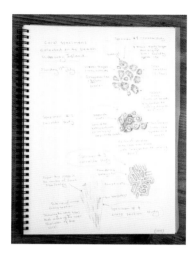

These broken coral fragments are from the beach on Hideaway island, Vanuatu. Since this is a marine sanctuary these coral skeleton specimens could not be taken off the island where I found them. Instead I took numerous photographs of the collection for my own records and did field sketches of the different corallite patterns. These sketches have since inspired several artworks.

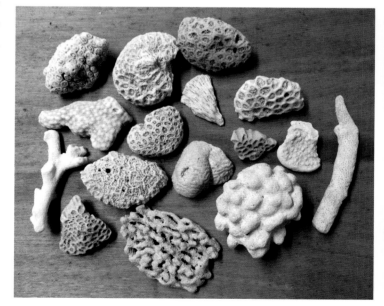

Collecting plant specimens

Tools and Materials:

- Zip-lock bags.
- Paper towels.
- Pruning shears or sharp scissors.
- Labels (sticky notes work well).
- Pencils or pens.

Method:

1. Select a healthy plant specimen. This may be a single flower, the tip of a branch, or an entire plant. Ensure that your specimen has all of the information you want to record. Photograph your specimen before it is removed from the plant.

2. Create a label for your specimen that records the name of the collector, date of collection, site of collection, and name of the plant (if known).

3. Cut the specimen with a pair of sharp scissors or pruning shears. Do not snap or bend the specimen off the plant, as this will do unnecessary damage.

4. Wrap the cut end of the specimen in some damp paper towel to help keep it moist and fresh.

5. Store the specimen and corresponding label in a clear zip-lock bag. Blow the bag up with your breath before sealing. The carbon dioxide from your breath will help to feed the specimen and keep it alive longer. The air will also act as padding to help protect your specimens from damage.

6. To extend the life of your fresh specimens, store them in their zip-lock bags, in the fridge.

Paper Nautilus

I was gifted a beautiful shell by a friend who knows that I like to collect such things. This shell was paper thin, translucent, and covered in a beautiful pattern of ridges and bumps. This curious specimen intrigued me, and following a bit of a research rampage I learned that it was in fact not a shell after all. This beautiful form is the egg case of an argonaut, or paper nautilus as it is more commonly known.

Not a lot is known about argonauts. They are rarely seen in the wild and have never been successfully kept in captivity. What we do know is that argonauts are pelagic octopuses and the females make these delicate egg cases with their specialized tentacles. The egg case is used as a brood chamber to house and protect her hundreds of eggs until they hatch. Like many octopuses, the argonaut has thousands of chromatophores in their skin. These allow the animal to change the color of its skin instantly to blend in with its surroundings or ward off predators. Argonauts have been photographed displaying many colors from soft grays through to vivid purple and orange tones. Unlike the true nautilus, an argonaut is not attached to her egg case and she can come completely out of it if threatened.

For my interpretation of an argonaut's egg case I focused on the beautiful ribbed pattern on the shell. Argonaut egg cases are mostly white, but I decided to portray mine in vivid oranges in reference to the bright colors the octopus can turn when disturbed. The embroidery was stitched as a single piece and shaped as it dried to mimic the natural curved shape of the egg case.

Kingdom: Animalia
Phylum: Mollusca
Class: Cephalopoda
Order: Octopoda
Family: Argonautidae
Genus: *Argonauta*
Species: *A. argo*

An Argonauta nodosa *egg case from my personal collection*

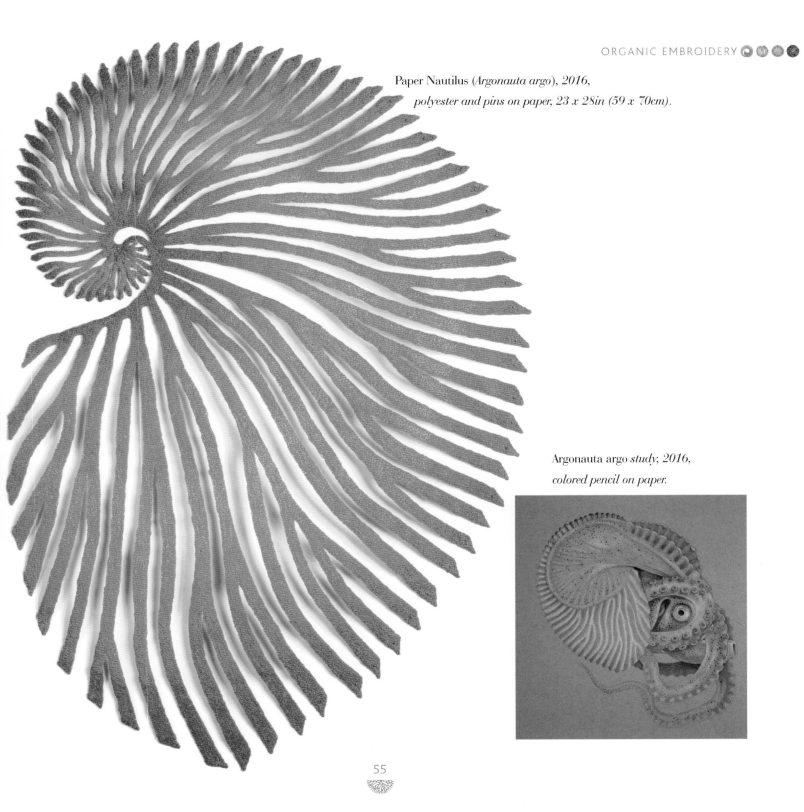

Paper Nautilus (*Argonauta argo*), *2016,*
polyester and pins on paper, 23 x 28in (59 x 70cm).

Argonauta argo *study, 2016,*
colored pencil on paper.

55

Preserving and displaying your specimen collection

My studio is littered with various natural objects I have acquired over the years. I find it very comforting and inspiring to be surrounded by these natural treasures. They act as reminders of my past fieldwork trips and they make excellent drawing references.

As you start to collect natural objects, it's a nice idea to create your own inspirational display. Robust objects such as shells, coral, bones, feathers, and seedpods do not need any special preservation or care. As long as they are stored in a safe, dry place they will continue to inspire for many years to come. More delicate natural objects, such as plants, will deteriorate over time if they are not preserved and cared for appropriately.

Plants specimens will change significantly when they die and dry out, so it is a good idea to photograph your specimens while they are fresh to capture their true character. One way to preserve plants is to press them flat.

I collected this little rainbow of leaves one day while out for a walk. Being very thin leaves they quickly wilted after being picked, so it was important to photograph them right away to capture their initial shape and colors.

I keep a collection of tiny natural fragments on display in an old typesetting drawer. I love to have parts of my collection around me when I work and this is a great way to show off the smaller and otherwise overlooked elements from the collection. In this drawer you will find shells, seedpods, bones, sea urchins, feathers, coral fragments, dried algae, and even the odd echidna quill.

Pressing plant specimens

Tools and Materials:

- Two wooden boards cut to the size of your pressing paper. Plywood or hardboard work well.
- Pressing paper: blotting paper and newspaper.
- Sheets of corrugated cardboard.
- Straps or heavy objects (bricks, phone books, etc.).

Method:

1. Build or buy a plant press that is large enough for your plant specimens. A press can be made simply with a pair of wooden boards cut to the size of the drying paper.
2. On one of the wooden boards, lay down a piece of corrugated card followed by a sheet of blotting paper and finally a sheet of newspaper.
3. Clean your specimen by removing any soil.
4. Arrange the specimen on the sheet of newspaper. Try to maintain the natural character of the plant with your arrangement.
5. Place another sheet of newspaper on top of the plant, followed by a sheet of blotting paper, then corrugated cardboard.
6. You can press several plant specimens at once. Each should be arranged in the same layers described above.
7. Cover with the top board. Lay heavy objects on top of the board or wrap the entire press tightly with straps. Ensure that pressure is applied evenly throughout the press. Store in a warm, dry place.
8. Check the press every few days and replace any damp paper with fresh sheets. Your specimens will take two to four weeks to completely dry.

Pressed plants can be mounted onto acid-free card stock to keep them flat and safe. The best way to attach your plants without damaging them is to affix them with little loops of dental floss stitched through the card and tied at the back. Plant specimens are fragile, so minimize handling these objects. Occasionally check your specimen collection for insect damage and mold growth.

Herbarium specimen, native violet (Viola hederacea).
This native violet has been pressed flat and attached to acid-free card with a loop of dental floss. The original color of the plant has changed significantly in the drying process, so my original color notation is very important if I wish to use this specimen for future study.

Typologies

Many of my pieces focus on a single natural structure in great detail. The *Typologies* project was different because it allowed me to explore many different structures within the one artwork. This wall installation is made up of 25 small nature studies each with a completely different focus. Inspired by the patterns, structures, and shapes found in plants, coral, cells, shells, and fossils, this installation brings together usually unrelated natural structures in the one artwork. The choice to create each piece in monochrome was a very conscious one. By removing the telltale color hints, the origins of many of the structures become obscured.

When these small studies are displayed together we naturally group them into patterns, forming connections between the structures. We begin to see the similarities and differences between the various organisms that make up our world. The series explores the balance, harmony, and interconnectivity of life on Earth.

Meredith installing Typologies.

Typologies, *2015, polyester thread, dimensions variable.*

Further Research

Fieldwork is a great way to collect primary material to inspire an artwork but this needs to be backed up with secondary research once back in the studio. Secondary research involves reading published literature about your nature finds to gain a deeper understanding of the organism. It may also involve sourcing extra imagery to build upon the visual material collected in the field. By learning all that you can about an organism, you will develop a detailed profile on your subject matter. This helps to develop a stronger final artwork.

The internet is a good place to start for generalized research, but scientific papers and publications will always provide the most accurate and comprehensive information. Research and study invariably uncovers environmental issues that are currently affecting the organism or its broader habitat. These issues can be useful in informing the conceptual side of an artwork.

Identification

Identification involves determining the scientific name (normally in Latin) for the things you find in nature. I always get great satisfaction out of knowing exactly what I have found in the field. Identifying your nature finds during or after fieldwork can enrich the entire nature study experience and it makes secondary research much easier. You can easily identify the things you find in nature with the right field guides and a bit of know-how.

Field guides are a great place to start your identification journey. They exist in a huge variety covering all forms of flora, fauna, and fungi. Their purpose is to help you identify what you find while out in nature. Field guides can be specific to a certain geographic area such as *Field Guide to the Native Plants of Sydney* or can be broad overviews such as *Seashells of the World*. I particularly like the old-fashioned paper field guides, but there are also some great, and very convenient, digital field guide "apps" available. Some guides are photographic references while others are illustrated. I prefer the illustrated guides because the drawings clearly show the important or unique elements of each species, plus the illustrations themselves are often very beautiful. Good field guides will have a key to help streamline identification.

Scientific identification may not be important to your own art projects, but I find that even a basic level of identification (to genus level) will give me a solid starting point for my investigations and it will streamline any secondary research.

Coast Pennywort

This piece is inspired by the venation system in a *Hydrocotyle bonariensis* leaf. Commonly known as the coast pennywort or Kurnell's curse, this plant is a perennial herb and in some places also a prolific weed. It is commonly found in sandy dunes near the beach and I often find myself picking a leaf or two to examine on my walks.

I have always loved the shape of this fleshy leaf with its intricate internal vein patterns. As with many leaves, if you hold a coast pennywort leaf up to the sunlight the delicate veins are lit up, revealing the spectacular beauty of its internal structure.

Kingdom: Plantae
Order: Apiales
Family: Araliaceae
Genus: *Hydrocotyle*
Species: *H. bonariensis*

Coast Pennywort
(*Hydrocotyle bonariensis*), 2015,
polyester thread and pins on paper,
29 x 26in (74 x 67cm).

Image research from books and the internet

Fieldwork helps to develop original visual resources but there may be times when you need or want to source alternate imagery. You may not be able to do the fieldwork yourself or you may wish to study a rare or exotic organism that you cannot experience firsthand. This is where the photographs, illustrations, and videos made by other people are valuable additions to your research.

Images can be sourced from books, magazines, and the internet. Whenever you work from the images of others it is important to consider the copyright of the imagery and be very careful not to infringe upon this. Always strive to create your own artwork designs and only use found imagery to inspire and inform your art. The work and images of other artists should never be flat out copied. This includes tracing your design off their imagery and recreating it in a different medium or style. Not only is this highly unethical, it can open you up to future prosecution.

If you want to use the imagery of others but are concerned about copyright infringement, you can explore imagery that is out of copyright. Copyright regulations differ from country to country but as a general rule an artwork or image is protected by copyright until 70 years after the author's death. Once copyright has lapsed the work is in the "public domain" and can be used by anyone. But, even if you are using an image that is out of copyright, it is good practice to acknowledge the original author.

Stock photography websites are good places to source imagery. The photographs on these sites are always high quality and you can purchase high-resolution versions of the

images for personal use. There are various licenses available with stock imagery and some of the extended licenses may permit the reproduction of imagery in artworks, but you will need to check this on a case-by-case basis.

Keep in mind that you can recreate another's artwork or image as a form of practice. Copying the artwork of another is a great way to learn new skills and techniques. Just ensure that any resulting artwork clearly references the original source and don't be tempted to exhibit these copies as your own artworks.

Ammonites

Ammonites are a group of extinct mollusks characterized by their spiraled shells. These ancient creatures are the ancestors of modern day cephalopods (squids, octopuses, cuttlefish) and are commonly found fossils. I have a small pyritized ammonite fossil in my collection of natural curiosities. This inspired my interest in these fascinating creatures of the past.

To develop my Red Ammonite design I used imagery of fossilized specimens from museum collections, mapping out the segmented spiral form, and redrawing it to suit my embroidery technique. Since only fossilized records of ammonites remain, we

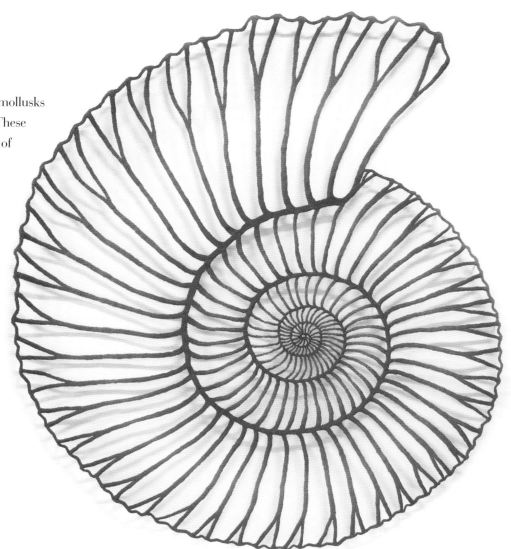

Ammonite museum specimens.

Red Ammonite, *2015, polyester thread and pins on paper, 37 x 39in (94 x 99cm).*

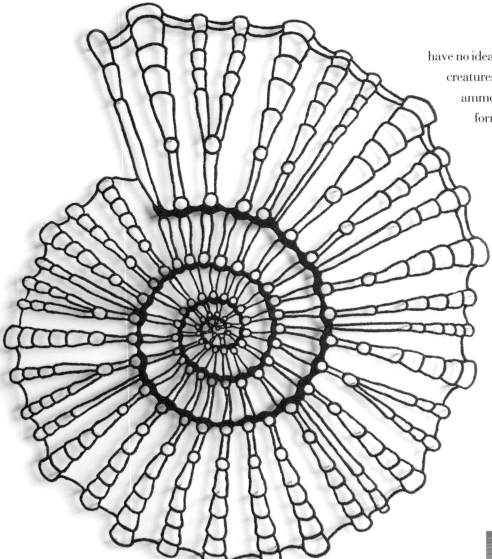

have no idea of the original coloring of these extraordinary creatures. So I took a bit of artistic license with my ammonite interpretation and stitched its beautiful form in vibrant red and orange threads.

The *Azure Ammonite* is inspired by one of my favourite natural history artists—Ernst Haeckel. The design is developed from a drawing on the ammonite page of his most famous publication, *Kunstformen der Natur* (Art Forms of Nature). Haeckel passed away in 1919 so his imagery is well out of copyright. His prints and illustrations are now freely available in the public domain. This makes it ethical to use his imagery as the basis for my *Azure Ammonite*.

Azure Ammonite, 2015 polyester thread and pins on paper, 36 x 41in (93 x 103cm).

Development of the design for the Azure Ammonite *based on Ernst Haeckel's illustrations.*

The art of keeping a sketchbook

Sketchbooks are wonderful places to explore and organize your thoughts and ideas. They are also places to make mistakes and to play. By keeping all of your research and creative thoughts in one place, over time you can build a valuable resource for your art making, while also assembling a beautiful collection of visual ideas and explorations.

Fieldwork sketchbooks

I use A4-sized sketchbooks for fieldwork. This size is large enough to be able to comfortably draw without feeling confined by the page, yet small enough to fit in a backpack. Spiral-bound sketchbooks are especially good for fieldwork because you can fold the cover back and lean on it to draw.

My fieldwork sketchbooks are not very pretty. They get dirty from being dropped on the ground and I don't take much pride on how the pages are laid out. They are simply a vehicle for collecting my observations, ideas, and fieldwork musings. There is nothing wrong with a messy sketchbook.

Nature journal

I compile the results of my fieldwork and research into a watercolor paper sketchbook that I call my Nature Journal. I take great care with this sketchbook and carefully plan out the composition of each page. Using a combination of pen, ink, and watercolor paints,

I have created a visual resource that assembles the most important imagery and written information from my studies of nature. This book is a culmination of all of my fieldwork and research presented in one place. I constantly refer back to this book when I am developing artwork designs. It is very precious to me.

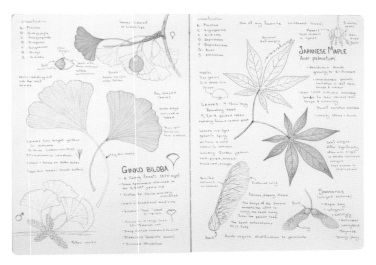

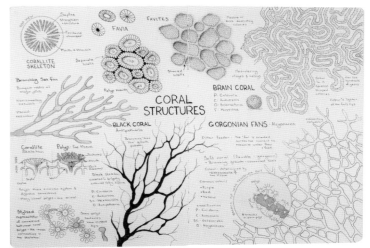

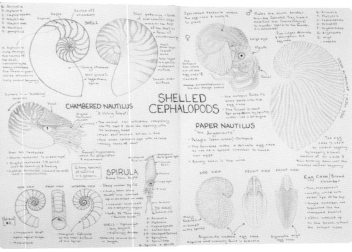

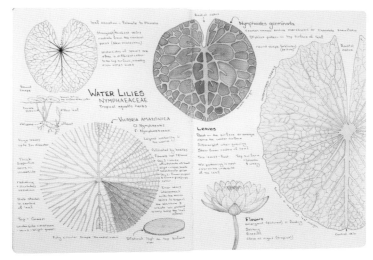

Amazonian Water Lily

Native to tropical South America, the Amazonian (or Victoria) water lily (*Victoria amazonica*) is a really impressive plant. Now used ornamentally around the world, it is characterized by its enormous circular leaves, which can grow up to seven feet (over two meters) across. These leaves can hold a significant amount of weight and small children are often photographed sitting on them like fairies. This waterlily also has a very interesting flowering process, where the flower completely changes color and sex over a 48-hour period.

Victoria amazonica's giant leaves and beautiful flowers are impressive, but for me, the most beautiful and fascinating part of this plant is the underside of its leaves. If you were to lift up one of the giant lily pads you would see a vibrant purple and green network of ribs. These look like thick tubes radiating out from the central stem. I focused on this amazing rib structure in my stitched interpretation of the Amazonian water lily.

Using historical photographs as reference, I drew the network of ribs so that they would fit inside a perfect circle. The main supportive ribs are depicted in dense stitching so that I could achieve a smooth color transition from vibrant purple on the outer edge of the leaf through to lime green in the center. The minor ribs, which connect the main ribs at regular intervals, are depicted with single lines of stitching, giving the piece a light airy feel.

This water lily is a great example of a natural structure that hides one of its most beautiful features away from view. I hope that my embroideries inspire people to look closer at nature and discover the beauty that is often hiding just under the surface.

Kingdom: Plantae
Clade: Angiosperms
Order: Nymphaeales
Family: Nymphaeaceae
Genus: *Victoria*
Species: *V. amazonica*

Amazonian Water Lily
(*Victoria amazonica*), 2015,
polyester thread and pins on paper,
27 x 27in (69 x 69cm).

Developing Artwork Designs for Embroidery

When you are developing any artwork you need to understand the possibilities and also the limitations of your medium, then keep these in mind while you design. This is especially important with the embroidery technique that we will be exploring in this book. The most important thing to remember with this technique is that the water-soluble base fabric is only a temporary surface. Once this material is removed, the embroidery may shift and change because its supporting base has gone. The removal of the base fabric is what makes this technique so exciting, but you need to design with this crucial structural change in mind if you want your artworks to be successful.

When developing an embroidery design, try to predict how the stitches will behave once the base fabric is removed. Curves, corners, spirals, and fine shapes may warp upon dissolving, so plan to address these issues in your design. Fine lines of stitching are the most likely to distort once the base fabric is removed. However, this distortion can be used to great creative effect—but it can also be frustrating when you want something to stay in a specific shape. Consider combining fine lines of stitching with some thicker areas. These dense areas of stitching will add strength to the design and help hold fine lines in place.

Dense areas of stitching can be used to support more delicate areas.
Red Coral Square, 2015, polyester thread and pins on paper,
28 x 28in (70 x 70cm).

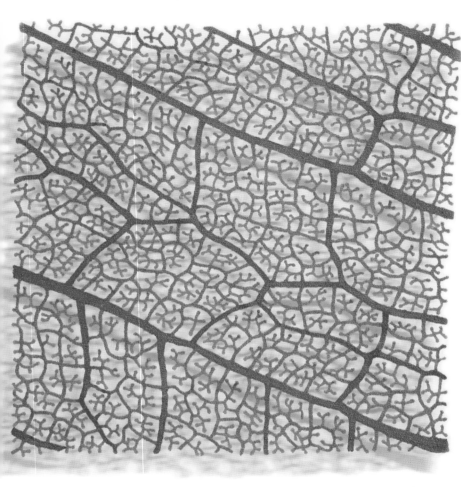

If your design is not connected it will fall apart when the base fabric is removed. To avoid this make sure that all of your lines of stitching overlap at some point in the design. Many of my artworks are inspired by structures in nature that have interconnecting growth systems, such as coral branches, or leaf veins. These structures make for very successful embroideries because they are so tightly connected that there is little room for distortion when the base fabric is dissolved and it has to stand alone.

Designs with lots of connection points are always very successful with this type of embroidery because they form a strong framework.
Orange Leaf Structure Square, *2015, polyester thread and pins on paper,*
28 x 28in (70 x 70cm).

Nautilus

Kingdom: Animalia
Phylum: Mollusca
Class: Cephalopoda
Order: Nautilida
Family: Nautilidae
Genus: *Nautilus*
Species: *N. pompilius*

The chambered nautilus (*Nautilus pompilius*) is probably the best-known shelled cephalopod. These creatures have fascinated me ever since I first saw one of their beautiful shells in a museum. I have since researched these shells and their unusual inhabitants extensively and created several artworks inspired by them. You could say that I have a bit of an obsession with the nautilus!

I have several nautilus shell specimens in my collection and they are my most prized shells. Working from these specimens and other imagery I have developed several designs that have evolved into embroidered artworks.

Design development images of nautilus shells.

My *Orange Nautilus* is an interpretation of the patterns on the external surface of the shell. This patterning is used as a type of camouflage in the wild and consists of deep orange bands that stripe across the otherwise white shell. My interpretation takes the striped pattern and expands it so that it covers the entire shell.

The internal chambers of a nautilus shell follow the mathematical formula of the logarithmic spiral. This growth spiral appears often in nature and the nautilus shell is often a first example given to anyone studying this marvelous spiral. If you were to cut a nautilus shell in half you would reveal the many chambers inside the shell. These chambers get progressively larger as they spiral out from the center of the shell. In the piece *Nautilus Unity* I demonstrate the perfection of this chambered growth pattern, depicting the internal chambers of two nautilus shells nestled together. The design borrows from the timeless balance of a ying-yang symbol.

Nautilus Unity, *2017, polyester thread and pins on paper, 21 x 27in (53 x 69cm).*

Orange Nautilus, *2013, polyester thread and pins on paper, 28 x 33in (70 x 85cm).*

Nautilus Unity *(detail).*

Nature Studies series

The *Nature Studies* series began as an exploration of various branching coral structures. It has since expanded to include any natural structure that interests me. Each of these designs is an individual framed artwork.

To create these pieces I start by tracing the inner ring of my embroidery hoop onto a blank piece of paper and then draw my design to fit within the confines of this circle. By using the same embroidery hoop for each piece, there is uniformity in the size of each artwork and thus the series. I often refer to the pages of my nature journal for reference when I develop these designs.

None of these designs are traced from a photograph—they are all drawn freehand. It is immensely satisfying to see a design grow organically rather than feeling the need to strictly copy a reference image. Once you understand a natural structure, how it forms, connects, and grows, you should be able to draw it without following your reference materials. You won't need to trace a photo; you can let your design grow as you draw, creating your own unique interpretation of nature.

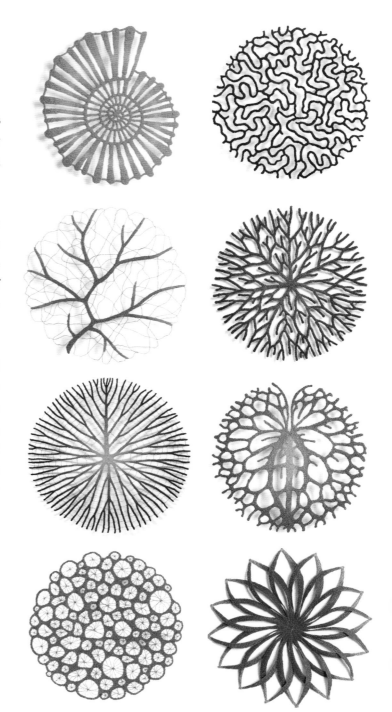

Developing a stitching plan

When developing embroidery designs, it is good practice to plan how you will physically build the embroidered drawing while at the sewing machine. You can do this by drawing a stitching plan. This plan will help to identify and, hopefully, solve any potential problems that may arise when embroidering.

Developing a stitching plan involves drawing your design on paper in the same way you hope to stitch the design at the sewing machine. This may seem like a laborious and unnecessary process but I find that it saves me a lot of time at the sewing machine and helps to avoid technical problems with an artwork. If you get the design right on paper first, then you know it will be a success when you recreate the design in embroidery. You won't need to draw a stitching plan for every project, only for designs that are complicated or if you are not sure where, or how, to start.

When developing your stitching plans consider the most effective way to do the drawing. If your design has several sections, or is made up of several colors, decide which layers of stitching will need to go down first to ensure the final design is seamlessly stitched and well constructed. If possible, complete the drawing so that it is made of a single continuous line. If you get the stitching plan right you will be able to stitch an entire section of the design without stopping and cutting the thread.

I always follow the same process to construct my embroideries. I lay down all of my single lines of stitching first, like a skeleton of the design. I make sure that this framework of stitches is well connected so that there is no chance of my final embroidery coming apart. I then add any denser areas of stitching on top of the stitched skeleton to solidify and strengthen the design. If I am changing or blending colors, I will work out where the best place to start stitching is, so that I don't go over any areas I have already stitched with a different color. All of these little considerations make for a neater final embroidered drawing.

Each artwork is different and will require a different approach to develop an effective stitching plan. How I draw and embroider is only one of many ways to approach a design. When planning your designs do what feels right for you. With ongoing practice you will develop sound drawing and stitching methods that will result in successful embroideries.

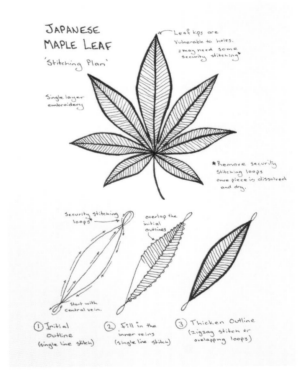

JAPANESE MAPLE LEAF
'Stitching Plan'

Single layer embroidery

Leaf tips are vulnerable to holes. May need some security stitching*

*Remove security stitching loops once piece is dissolved and dry.

Security stitching loops

overlap the initial outlines

Start with central vein.

① Initial Outline (single line stitch)

② Fill in the inner veins (single line stitch)

③ Thicken Outline (zigzag stitch or overlapping loops)

Japanese Maple

There was a beautiful Japanese maple tree in the front yard of the house where I grew up. In fall the leaves of this tree went through a stunning color transformation from their usual green, through vibrant shades of yellow and orange, until they finally settled on blood red. I remember collecting so many of those leaves as a child and I still occasionally find them stuffed into the pages of my childhood books.

I have created several artworks inspired by that maple. I started with individual leaf studies, trying to capture the changing colors and their delicate veining networks. I then moved on to whole leafy branches. But I feel like I have only scratched the surface of this subject. I fully expect that there will be many maple leaf artworks in my future.

Kingdom: Plantae
Clade: Angiosperms
Order: Sapindales
Family: Sapindaceae
Genus: *Acer*
Species: *A. palmatum*

3

1. Maple Leaves, *2015, polyester thread and pins on paper.*
2. Maple Leaf Study, *2015, polyester thread and pins on paper, 16 x 16in (40 x 40cm).*
3. Maple Branch, *2015, polyester thread and pins on paper, 30 x 24in (75 x 62cm).*
4. Maple Branch, *detail.*

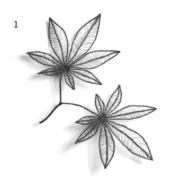

1

2

2

2

Going large

Your embroidery designs need not be limited to what you can fit inside an embroidery hoop. Go as large as you dare. Big embroideries are a great way to build complex designs and they are especially good for designs with lots of fine lines. Many of my leaf embroideries become larger pieces so that I can include every minor vein in the design.

When planning a large work I find it easier to draw a smaller version of the design in my sketchbook and then enlarge this onto a big sheet of paper. By getting the design right in my sketchbook first I save lots of time fiddling with a large drawing. When enlarging a design it can be difficult to keep the correct proportions if you are redrawing the design freehand. It is helpful to use a digital or overhead projector to shine your design on a wall first. You can then trace the design onto a sheet of paper and this scaled drawing will become the template for your artwork.

Once the design is finalized on paper it can be traced onto a sheet of water-soluble fabric with permanent markers. The design is then ready to be taken to the sewing machine for embroidery.

I use an overhead projector to enlarge my designs. I think I am probably one of the few people who still use this old technology. A digital projector would probably do the job just as easily; but I like my trusty old overhead and it has served me well. I will be heartbroken if the bulb ever blows and I can't find a replacement. Here are some examples of large artwork designs on paper (far right).

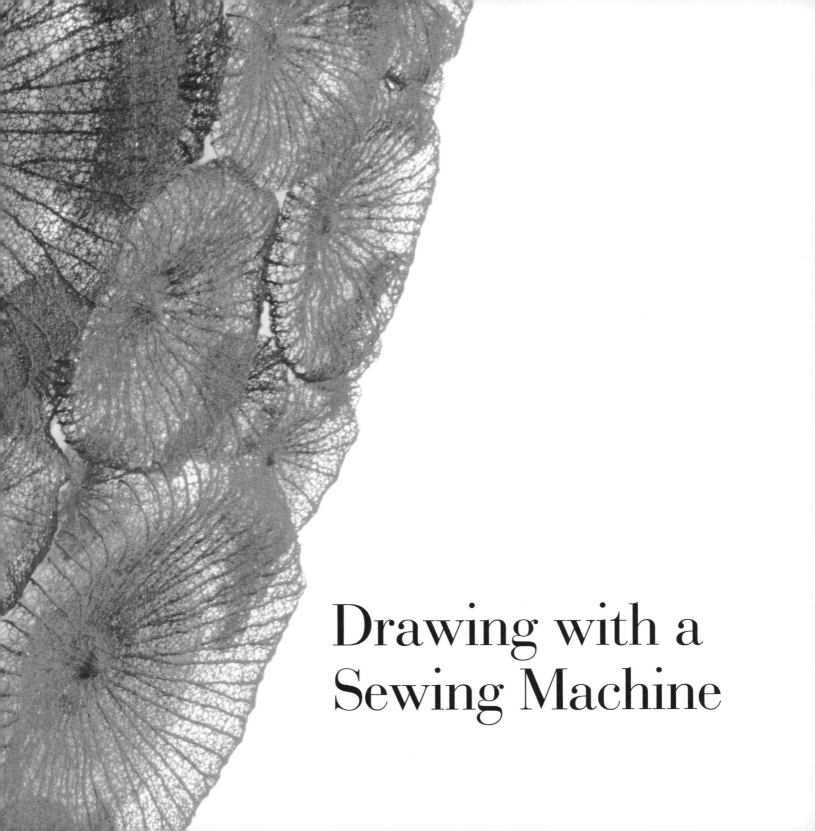

Drawing with a
Sewing Machine

The embroidery process I use is not a fancy, new, or difficult technique. It is simply a more creative use of darning, a common patch-mending process. For this type of embroidery the sewing machine is stripped back to its most basic settings. The feed dogs (drop feed) are turned off and this allows for free movement of fabric under the needle so you can move, and therefore draw, in any direction. This creative use of the darning process is commonly referred to as "freehand machine embroidery."

Another element that makes my artworks possible is the revolutionary base fabric that I sew onto. This fabric is water-soluble and acts as a temporary surface for the stitched drawing. Once the drawing is complete this material is washed away leaving just the skeleton of stitches behind. The result is embroidery that is liberated from the boundaries of a base cloth and allowed to morph into a more sculptural object.

The following chapter outlines the freehand machine embroidery technique and describes various ways you can approach this way of drawing with your sewing machine.

This type of embroidery will feel a bit strange at first. It is the equivalent of moving a sheet of paper rather than a pencil to do a drawing. Approach this new way of stitching with playfulness and freedom. Embrace the scribble and the squiggle. Don't worry about staying within the lines and above all have fun. It is only through experimentation and play that we can discover our own creative voice.

Tools and Materials

Sewing machines

The freehand embroidery technique can be done on almost any domestic sewing machine. As long as you have the ability to drop the feed dogs you can stitch freehand with the machine.

Some other features that will improve your freehand sewing experience, but are not essential, include:

- A long machine arm to allow for larger projects and ease of movement.
- Fast stitching speed.
- Bright lights built into the machine.
- A slide-on, free arm, extension table.

If you are looking to buy a sewing machine my advice is to purchase the absolutely best machine you can currently afford. Quality

machines are expensive, but they should be seen as an investment. A good quality machine, if well maintained, should last a lifetime.

Darning or freehand embroidery foot

Most domestic sewing machine brands have their own style of freehand embroidery or darning feet. These feet commonly have a small circle, oval, or horseshoe-shaped foot and they do not sit flat on the sewing bed when the presser foot is lowered. These feet allow free movement of the fabric under the foot.

Darning or freehand embroidery feet are not standard, so they may have to be purchased separately. If you cannot source a freehand or darning foot to fit your machine you can still do freehand machine embroidery. Simply remove the foot altogether and keep your fingers out of the way when you embroider. Make sure that you still put the presser foot down so that you have top thread tension when you work.

Machine embroidery hoop

I always work with an embroidery hoop to keep the work flat and taut to prevent distortion when stitching. A good quality embroidery hoop with a tight grip is important. Personally I prefer the wooden machine hoops because they are more rigid than hand embroidery hoops. Machine hoops also have a thinner profile so they fit under the machine foot.

Embroidery scissors

For trimming threads while working. A good pair will last a lifetime.

Machine needles

Make sure your needle is sharp, straight, and changed frequently. I personally use sharps (or jeans) needles, size 80–90.

Water-soluble stabilizer

There is a large range of water-soluble fabric available on the market, but not all varieties are suitable for this type of freehand embroidery. I like to work with a non-woven water-soluble fabric that is made from PVA. It is white in color and looks like a thin sheet of interfacing. There are many different brand names for this material, which can be a bit confusing, but they are all pretty much the same product. Some popular brand names include Vilene 541, Solusheet, Soluweb, Legacy/Pellon: Wash-N-Gone, Floriani: Wet-N-Gone, and MacRinse.

There is a clear, plastic, film-style water-soluble fabric available on the market, often called Romeo or Solvi. I have not been as successful with this material because I find it tears easily during hooped stitching.

Machine threads

Threads come in a huge variety of thicknesses, types, and colors, which will all give different visual and tactile results. Your choice of threads depends entirely upon your project and preferences, but make sure that whatever thread you use is strong and reliable: a poor quality or old thread will break repeatedly and be very frustrating and annoying to work with.

I predominantly use polyester machine embroidery thread because it is a strong thread that has a lovely soft luster when stitched. Polyester is also more archival than natural fibers, which being organic, can break down and fade over time.

Getting Started

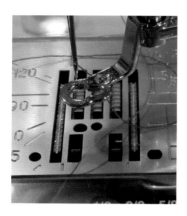 

Machine setup

1. Turn feed dogs off.
2. Insert darning/freehand embroidery foot.
3. Set machine for straight stitch (stitch width to 0).
4. Thread your top thread as normal.
5. Thread your bobbin.

Note: If your bobbin case has a finger with a hole in it, thread this hole for extra tension control.

Starting off/Locking stitches

1. Stretch a single sheet of water-soluble fabric in an embroidery hoop. It should be nice and tight like a drum.
2. Place the hoop, fabric side down, on your sewing bed. Using the sewing machine hand wheel, pull the bobbin thread up through the top of the fabric.
3. Sew a few stitches to secure your thread and trim off both top and bottom thread ends close to the fabric.

You are now ready to start drawing with your machine. To do this, simply run the machine and move the hoop around the needle to create various marks and lines. It is as simple as that.

Freehand work can feel a bit strange at first but with practice and dedication you will soon refine your new drawing skills and stitch with confidence. There are no strict rules when it comes to this way of drawing so play with it and have fun.

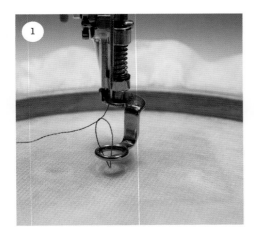

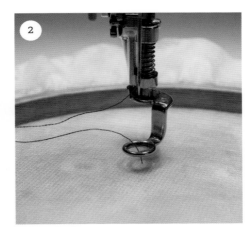

Getting Started
1. *Pull up bottom thread.*
2. *Both threads on top.*
3. *Lock stitches on the spot.*
4. *Trim threads.*
5. *Ready to go!*

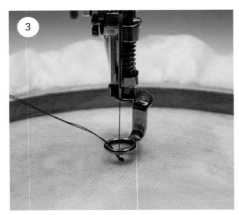

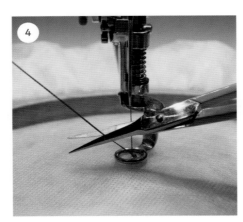

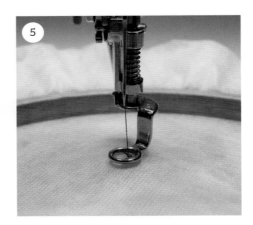

Single-Line Stitching

One of the quickest ways to build up a drawing with freehand machine embroidery is to create a design from single lines of stitching. This approach is good for creating delicate, lace-like pieces and scribbly sketches in thread.

With single-line drawing there is an emphasis on planning how you will construct the embroidery to ensure its success. You want to develop a design that will hold together in a predictable manner and not unravel or fall apart once the base fabric is removed. A good rule of thumb is to create a design that has lots of connection points or lines that overlap. The more connections you have in your stitched drawing, the more strength your structure will have.

The best way to plan for a single-line drawing is to physically draw the design on paper first. By developing a sound stitching plan you can avoid problems while sewing.

When you are stitching a single-line drawing pay special attention to the placement of your lines and where they overlap and connect. Go slow and steady to make sure your lines land exactly where you want them. To check your connections try holding your embroidery up to a light source. This will illuminate your stitching and help to identify any thin or missing problem areas.

Stitching the Maidenhair Study.
I approached this piece by stitching the individual leaves first, jumping my stitches from one leaf to the next. I then went back in to fill in the darker stem.

Maidenhair Study, *2017, polyester thread,*
8 x 6in (20 x 15cm).

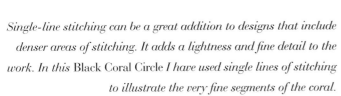

Single-line stitching can be a great addition to designs that include
denser areas of stitching. It adds a lightness and fine detail to the
work. In this Black Coral Circle *I have used single lines of stitching*
to illustrate the very fine segments of the coral.

Scribble sheet

Creating a scribble sheet is a good way to get familiar with freehand embroidery and helps to develop the fine motor skills needed to draw confidently with your sewing machine. A scribble sheet is simply a mass of stitched lines that build up an interconnected structure. By looping and overlapping single lines of stitching you can quickly create sheets of lace-like fabric.

When you dissolve the base fabric, the glue from the water-soluble stabilizer will absorb into the threads, harden, and then stick the fibers together. You can then cut shapes out of the fabric you have created and the edges will not fray or unravel. Scribble sheets can also be molded and stretched into various shapes. The possibilities are endless.

Method:

1. Set up the machine for freehand embroidery, stitch a few stitches to lock your threads in place, then trim off the thread ends. Move the embroidery hoop in small circles creating loops of stitched lines. Ensure that your loops overlap and interconnect to form a consistent structure. It doesn't matter if the loops are uniform in shape and size, or irregular; as long as they all connect, your structure will hold together.

2. Wash away the base fabric and let the embroidery dry completely. (Not shown.)

3–8. Using sharp scissors, cut out any shape you desire.

1

Stitched Letters

Writing with stitch is a great way to further develop the fine motor skills needed for accurate freehand embroidery. It is a quick, fun way to create an embroidered drawing using the single line stitching technique.

As an experimental side project I set myself a challenge to stitch a piece of text every day over the span of one month. I would start each day in the studio by drawing up the page lines of that day's "note" and then spend anywhere between ten minutes to an hour stitching down my thoughts. Some days I wrote myself long letters. Other days a short poem. Sometimes I just wrote myself a to-do list for the day. Overall I found the process therapeutic; it was a great way to loosen up before a day of otherwise much slower and denser stitching jobs.

The strange beauty of this series was that once the base fabric was washed away the text distorted and became unreadable. So my thoughts and personal letters remained a secret!

Stitched Letters, *2013, polyester thread, various dimensions.*

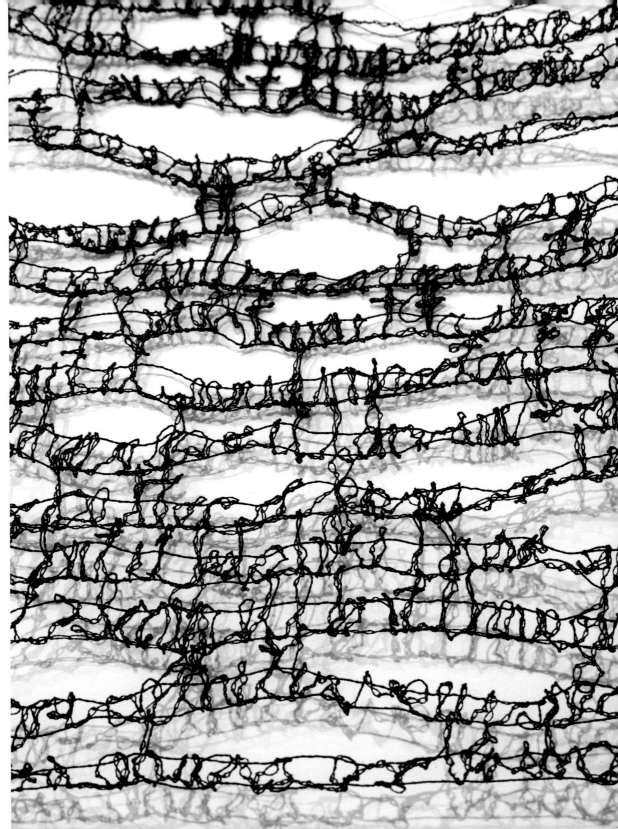

Dense Stitching

Most of my artworks are characterized by very dense areas of stitching where the individual stitches are almost hidden because they are so tightly knotted together. This density helps the pieces keep their shape once the base fabric is washed away and it provides a lovely subtle surface texture. Dense stitching can be used to create lines of stitches or fill in larger areas to form a mat of stitching. It also provides opportunities to seamlessly blend colors. It is a very versatile way to work.

There are several ways to build up dense areas in a stitched drawing, just like there are several ways to shade a pencil drawing. My advice is to keep experimenting and playing until you develop a way to stitch that feels right for you. As long as your stitches are well connected and you build a tight and secure structure, your embroidery will hold together once the base fabric is dissolved.

When I stitch dense areas in my artwork I sew in a series of overlapping loops. These loops are stitched so tightly together that you can barely see any gaps in the stitching. I find this to be a good way to build up both the thin lines of stitching and to fill in the larger areas.

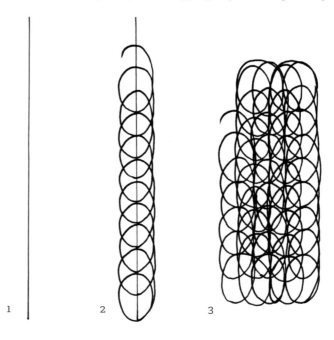

Dense stitching using the overlapping loops stitching technique.

1   2   3

Method:

1. Draw a straight line to act as a guideline.

2. Stitch over the guideline in small, overlapping loops to form a solid line of dense stitching.

3. The overlapping loops technique can be used to build up larger areas of dense stitching. Just keep building the structure with loops that interconnect.

Note: These illustrations are expanded views of the overlapping loops stitching technique so that you can clearly see how your stitches should be laid down. When stitching with this technique, aim to draw very small loops only a few millimeters in size. You want your loops to tightly overlap to form a dense structure.

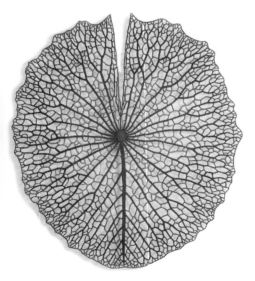

Dense stitching using the overlapping
loops stitching technique.

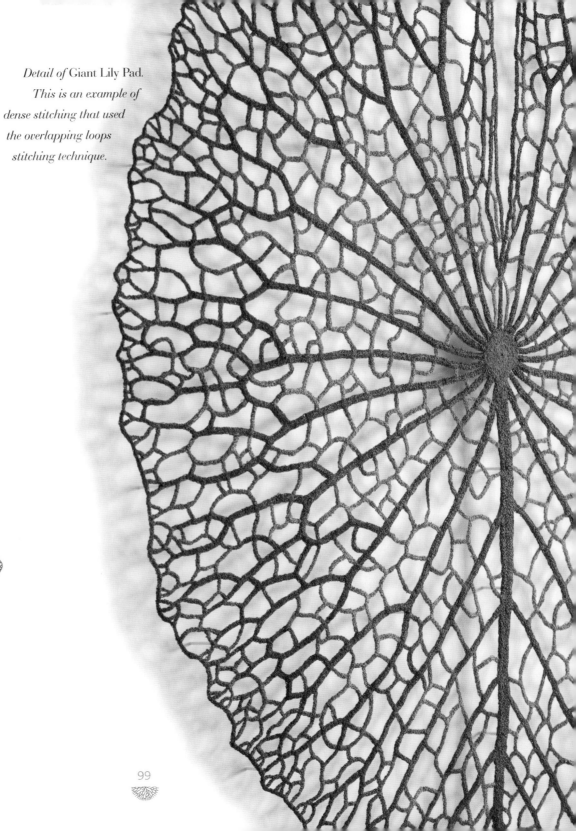

Detail of Giant Lily Pad.
This is an example of
dense stitching that used
the overlapping loops
stitching technique.

Giant Lily Pad, 2015, polyester thread and
pins on paper, 37 x 41in (93 x 103cm).

Red Cabbage, *2014,*
polyester thread,
35 x 35in (90 x 90cm).

Red Cabbage *(details) before the*
base fabric was washed away.

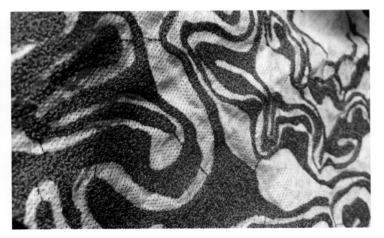

Red Cabbage

Kingdom: Plantae
Order: Brassicales
Family: Brassicaceae
Genus: *Brassica*
Species: *B. oleracea*

While I am not a big fan of eating cabbage, I have always loved cutting them up. The brain-like lines of swirling purple that are revealed when you slice into a red cabbage are like little natural labyrinths and I find them incredibly beautiful.

Several years ago I was asked to be a part of a group exhibition that combined food and art in a beautiful way. Twenty artists from around the world were invited to each create an artwork inspired by a piece of fresh produce (fruit, vegetable, spice, etc.). I chose the red cabbage for its beautiful fractal-like patterning. It was a great excuse to cut up a pile of these humble vegetables as I developed my design.

This piece was stitched using the overlapping loop technique to create an even mat of dense stitching. This technique allowed me to stitch both thick and thin lines to form a cohesive design.

Painting with stitch

The first pieces I ever created with the freehand machine embroidery technique were thread paintings. These were densely stitched designs, with none of the characteristic negative space that you see in my work today. I was essentially creating my own unique fabrics made entirely from embroidery.

My initial goal with these pieces was to create stitched versions of some small watercolor paintings I had made. Being completely new to the freehand embroidery technique, I began playing and drawing with the threads. I stitched without much of a plan and really had no idea how it would turn out. I approached the embroidery in much the same way as I would a traditional painting, putting down layers of color, just using threads rather than paint. I started by filling in the "paper" of my painting in light cream thread, and then began to add layers of darker threads until I had completed my stitched painting and created a solid mat of stitches. I stitched by drawing lots of tight squiggles and swirls in thread. This looped way of stitching felt very natural to me at the time and I still work in a similar manner today.

I only made a few of these thread paintings before I moved onto more lace-like stitching approaches. On these pages are some of my favorite early pieces. I learned so much while making them.

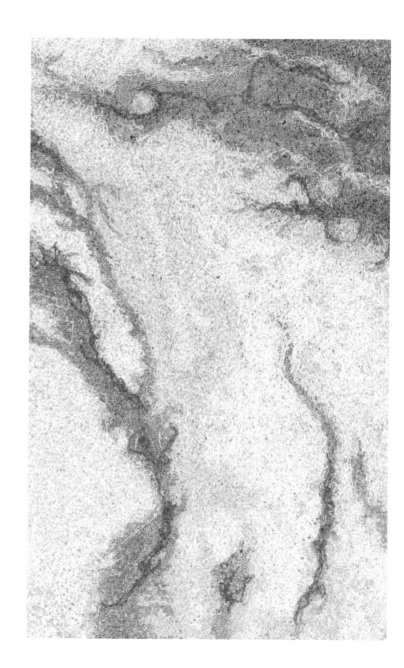

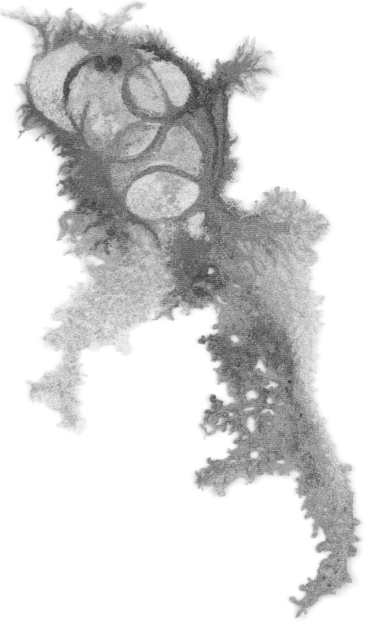

Zigzag Stitching

Using the zigzag setting on your machine is a great way to build up thin lines of stitching that are a consistent thickness. Straight or slightly curved lines work best with this technique. Rounded shapes and tight corners are a bit more of a challenge, but can be achieved with practice and patience.

Be warned that a standard zigzag line will unravel once the base fabric is washed away. This can, however, be avoided by building up a thick line of zigzag with many overlapping stitches.

Method:

1. Draw a single line of straight stitching to act as a guideline for your zigzag.
2. Set your stitch width to a narrow zigzag (0.1 inch or 2–3 millimeters). Wider zigzag settings are likely to tear your base fabric and ruin the project.
3. Moving slowly and steadily, stitch over your guideline with a zigzag stitch so that the stitches are very close together, similar to a satin stitch.
4. Once you have completed your line of stitching, go back over the zigzag in the opposite direction, stitching over the line you just stitched. This will produce a narrow tube of tight stitches that will not unravel once the base fabric is removed.

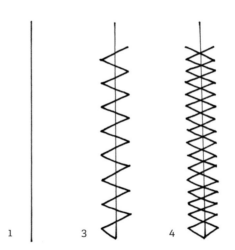

Note: *This illustration is an expanded view of the zigzag stitching technique so that you can see how your stitches should ideally land when you sew. Aim for a very tightly stitched zigzag line when you work, like a satin stitch.*

Leaves with zigzag edges

A zigzag stitch is a great way to create neat, smooth edges on shapes. This dense stitching adds body to the embroidery, creating a firm outline that will support the form once the base fabric is dissolved. This activity uses a combination of single-line stitching and zigzag edging to create delicate leaf shapes.

Method:

1. Draw a leaf shape outline with a single line of stitching. Start with the mid-vein then loop back to draw the outer edge of the leaf blade.

2. Fill in the center of the leaf with a single-line stitched pattern. In this example I have stitched straight lines that mimic the secondary vein pattern often seen in leaves, but feel free to stitch any design you like. Ensure that the lines of your inner leaf pattern overlap the leaf outline. This will guarantee that your design will hold together once the base fabric is dissolved.

3. Set the desired stitch width to start zigzag stitching. In this example I have used 0.1 of an inch (2.5mm) width. Stitch over the mid-vein with a tight zigzag stitch. Move slowly and steadily so that the stitches land right next to each other, similar to a satin stitch.

4. Go back over your line of stitches with a second line of tight zigzag stitches. This double layering of the zigzag will help ensure that all of your stitches are well connected and will stay together once the underlying fabric is dissolved.

5. Stitch the outer edge of the leaf using the same zigzag process described above.

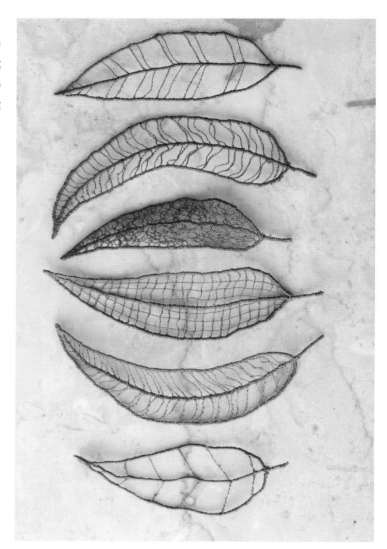

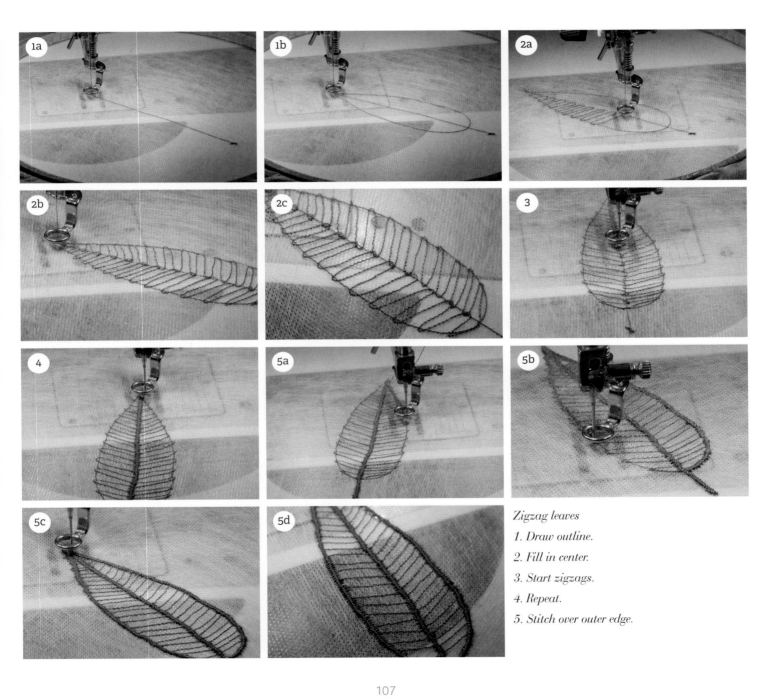

Zigzag leaves

1. *Draw outline.*
2. *Fill in center.*
3. *Start zigzags.*
4. *Repeat.*
5. *Stitch over outer edge.*

The New Neighbours

Kingdom: Animalia
Phylum: Cnidaria
Class: Anthozoa
Order: Corallimorpharia
Family: Discosomatidae
Genus: *Discosoma*

Discosoma, or as they are more commonly known, mushroom corals, are a tropical marine animal similar to soft coral. They often exist in large colonies, overlapping each other as they grow and propagate. I have been making artworks inspired by the beautiful fleshy forms of *Discosoma* for years. I love the beautiful radiating patterns on the surface of their oral disks and the organic shapes they make as they grow over the top of each other.

The New Neighbours, *2017,*
polyester thread, dimensions variable.

My wall installation *The New Neighbours* is made up of over 400 individual embroideries mimicking the color, shape, and structural patterning of a common *Discosoma* species. The work explores the issues surrounding global warming and the impending changes that the world's reefs will face over the next few decades. In the face of these changes to our coral I began studying species that may survive and thrive in warmer oceans. Colonies of corallimorphs have been known to rapidly cover empty spaces in a reef, like a living carpet over coral rubble. Species from this order are hardy, fast-growing organisms that are resistant to pollution, water acidity, and temperature changes, making them potential survivors of the impending reef destruction.

I purposely kept the individual elements of this installation very open and lace-like so that the overlapping in the final composition would build up the depth of the work. I began each piece by drawing the radiating veins of the *Discosoma* oral disk with a zigzag stitch. A fine mesh of stitches was then laid over the entire circular shape. After dissolving the base fabric the pieces were draped over molds to give them a unique shape, further referencing the natural character of mushroom coral and its remarkable structures.

Thinking in Layers

An embroidered drawing is already somewhat three-dimensional, but a multilayered design will add extra depth and interest to an artwork. Multilayered pieces may look very complicated and difficult to make, but they simply require a bit of planning before you start stitching.

Violet Sea Whip, *2017, polyester thread, 22 x 29in (57 x 74cm).*

This *Violet Sea Whip* is an example of an artwork that is multilayered. The initial drawn design had several overlapping sections that would not have been possible to create in a single-stitched drawing. To resolve this issue the embroidery was stitched as two separate, but similar layers. These two layers were stitched together at a planned connection point prior to dissolving the base fabric.

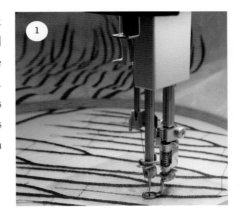
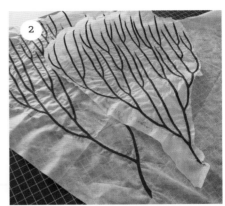
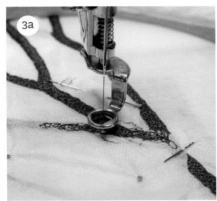
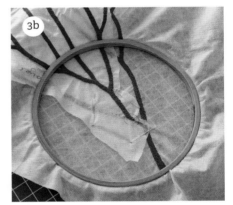

1. *Stitching* Violet Sea Whip.
2. *The two layers.*
3. *Stitching the two layers together.*
4. *Final artwork prior to dissolving.*

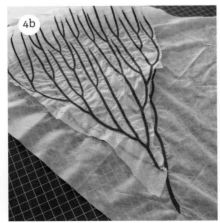
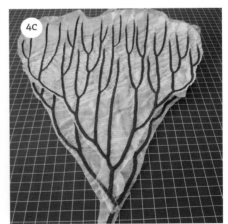

Color Blending

When working with traditional mediums like paint, one can mix up infinite hues, shades, and tones. But when it comes to drawing with threads we are limited to the colors that the threads come in. To help overcome these color limitations I developed a way to blend the colors together while stitching.

My color-blending technique focuses on fine-tuning the thread tension so that both the top and bottom (bobbin) threads are visible on one side of the embroidery. I find that the colors blend more evenly on the underside of the embroidery. The topside of my embroidery becomes the underside of the finished artwork.

When working in this way the bottom (or bobbin) thread color will be the most dominant color in the blend. The top thread tension can be tweaked to bring more or less of the top thread down to the underside of the drawing, introducing specks of the secondary color. With the introduction of these specks of top thread color into the underside of the embroidery, the eye blends the colors together, much like a pointillist painting.

Top side of the embroidery.
(Back of the final artwork.)

Underside of the embroidery.
(Front of the final artwork.)

Here you can see both sides of my Leaf Venation Study. *On the top side the color transitions are very obvious. However, on the underside of the embroidery (the top of the artwork) the colors blend in a much more subtle and natural way.*

Top side showing the obvious color changes.

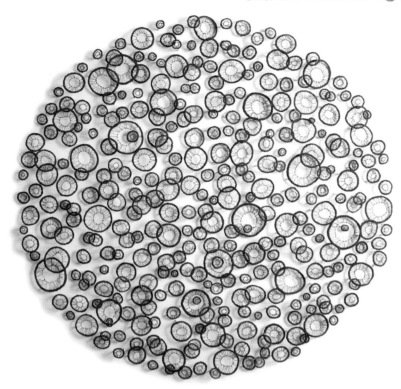

Under the Microscope, *2015, polyester thread and pins on paper, 37 x 37in (93 x 93cm).*

The underside (bobbin side) is much more nuanced.

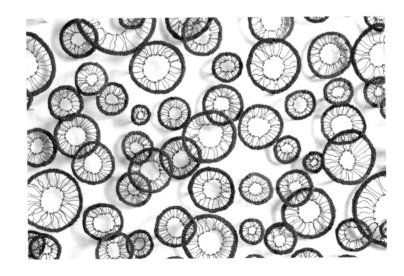

In this little color blend swatch I explored the subtle blue shades that could be achieved by using only one color in the bobbin thread and three different blues on the top. This resulted in a subtle fading shift in blue tones on the underside of the embroidery.

Color blend strip

A color blend strip will illustrate the new colors that can be achieved by blending two threads together. Once you understand the various color-blending possibilities and how to achieve them, you can make smooth transitions between thread colors in your embroideries. Before you begin any color blending ensure that your thread tension is correctly set for color blending (see page 112 for more information on this).

Top thread	Bobbin thread
Color 1	Color 1
Color 2	Color 1
Color 1	Color 2
Color 2	Color 2

Top side.

Underside (bobbin side).

Method:

1. Thread your machine with color 1 in both the top and bobbin thread. Stitch a small section of dense embroidery. I find that the overlapping loop stitching approach works well for color blending, but feel free to use whatever approach works best for you.

2. Replace the top thread with color 2 and stitch a second section of dense embroidery next to the first. Slightly overlap the stitching so that the cells connect and the colors merge even more.

3. Replace the top thread with color 1 again. Replace the bobbin thread with color 2. Stitch a third section of dense embroidery next to the second.

4. Replace the top thread color with color 2, and stitch a final section of dense embroidery next to the third layer.

Want the colors to blend on the top side of the embroidery?

It is possible to blend colors on the top side of the embroidery, but I find that the result is not as gradual as the underside method. If you do want to experiment with color blending on the top side, follow the same sequence described at left, but swap the order of the top and bobbin thread transitions.

Want to add more colors?

Just continue your strip following the same sequence to introduce your new colors.

Top of embroidery.

Underside of embroidery (bobbin side).

Caladium

I have always loved caladiums. There are many varieties of these common houseplants available, including some unique cultivars that are bred for their vibrant leaf coloring. This piece was inspired by one such cultivar, a caladium bi-color, commonly known as "Thai Beauty." The leaves of this plant have a unique patterning comprising red, white, and green segments.

This artwork is a good example of blended complementary colors. Using the color blending process just described, even opposite hues or colors, like this red and green, can be seamlessly blended together.

Kingdom: Plantae
Order: Alismatales
Family: Araceae
Subfamily: Aroideae
Genus: *Caladium*

Caladium, 2016, polyester thread and pins on paper, 26 x 32in (66 x 82cm).

Color blend grid

A color blend grid swatch is a great activity for exploring the blending possibilities of several thread colors in the one swatch. Your finished swatch should have lines of your top thread color going in one direction and lines of the bobbin thread color going in the opposite direction on the underside of the swatch. For this demonstration I have worked with four colors but you can use more or fewer colors if you like—simply expand or shrink the grid as needed. Try blending very different colors together in these grids. You may be surprised at the wonderful color possibilities you achieve.

Method:

1. Select a range of colors that you want to blend and fill a bobbin with each color. Ensure that your thread tension on the machine is set for optimum color blending (page 156).

2. Draw a grid on your water-soluble fabric to use as a guide when you are stitching your swatch. The squares in this example each measure 0.4 inches (1 x 1cm).

3. Thread the top and bobbin threads with color 1. Stitch the first cell of your swatch using a dense stitching technique.

4. Change your top thread to color 2 and stitch a second cell right next to the first slightly overlapping the stitching so that the cells connect.

5. Repeat step 4, adding a new top thread color for each new cell, until you have used all of your chosen colors and created a row or column of stitched cells.

6. Rethread your top thread with color 1 and swap the bobbin thread to color 2. Stitch a second row of stitched cells directly above the first, following the same top thread color order you used for the first row. Overlap the cells slightly so that they connect.

7. Continue to stitch rows for all the remaining bobbin colors.

Color grid stitching sequence

Top Threads				Bobbin Threads			
4	4	4	4	1	2	3	4
3	3	3	3	1	2	3	4
2	2	2	2	1	2	3	4
1	1	1	1	1	2	3	4

1

2
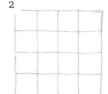

3

4

5a

5b
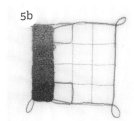

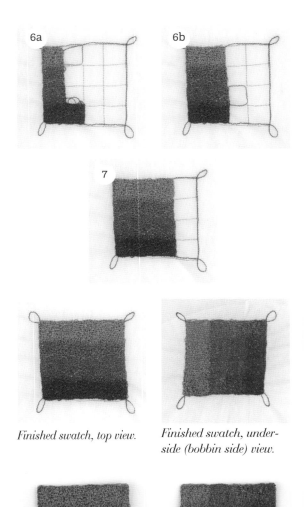

6a

6b

7

Finished swatch, top view.

Finished swatch, under-side (bobbin side) view.

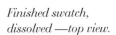

Finished swatch, dissolved —top view.

Finished swatch, dissolved—underside/ bobbon side view.

By blending similarly toned thread colors you can create an almost seamless gradation of color.

Leaf Lines

The *Leaf Lines* were developed during an artist residency in Port Macquarie, NSW, Australia. I lived and worked in this area throughout the residency, drawing upon the local environment for my inspiration. During my initial fieldwork I ended up in a national park. While searching for inspiration I was drawn to the subtle rainbow of color underfoot. This easily overlooked spectacle was made up of fallen eucalypt leaves in various stages of drying and decomposing. I collected a range of them and took them into the studio to inform my work.

Inspired by my rainbow of leaves, color became my focus for the residency. I had a range of thread that closely matched the colors of my collected leaves, but none were exact. To explore the color possibilities of my chosen threads I created a color swatch grid. The grid sampled 14 thread colors, exploring the various color combinations that could be achieved by stitching these threads together. This grid was used as a reference to inform my thread color choices over the residency.

During my time in Port Macquarie I stitched dozens of small leaf studies inspired by my collected eucalypt leaves. These studies explored the many colors that could be achieved by blending my range of threads together. These individual leaves were eventually turned into two "sister" artworks that I called the *Leaf Lines*. Each line is like a color gradient, celebrating the beautifully subtle range of colors these leaves produce.

Leaf Line #1, *2017, polyester thread and pins on paper, 17 x 62in (44 x 157cm).*

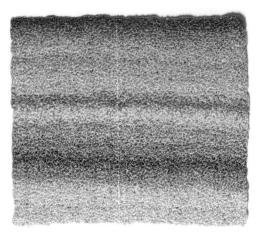

Top view of the eucalypt thread swatch grid.

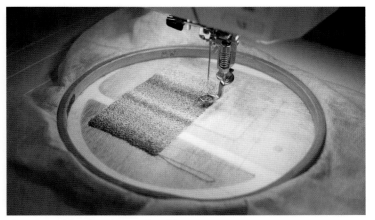

Top view of the thread swatch grid.

Bottom (bobbin) view of the thread swatch grid.

Completed thread swatch grid in my sketchbook with the thread samples.

Leaf Line #2, 2017, polyester thread and pins on paper, 17 x 62in (44 x 157cm).

Dissolving
and
Sculpting

The Dissolving Process

My favorite part of this art-making practice is the moment when the base fabric is washed away and my stitched drawing comes to life. This is when the magic happens: the embroidery is transformed—it becomes sculptural and takes on a life of its own.

Removing water-soluble fabric from your stitched drawing is very simple. The base fabric will quickly melt away in hot water and transform from a solid sheet of fabric to a sticky glue-like substance within a second or two. The water-soluble fabric hardens like glue as it dries, adding structure and stability to the embroidery. So, when I dissolve the base fabric from my embroideries, I aim to trap some of the water-soluble fabric within the thread fibers. You can mold, shape, and manipulate the embroidery during the drying process. As the sculpture dries it will retain its new molded form.

This chapter discusses the various dissolving methods that I use, offering suggestions you can apply to your own creations. I also explore ways to mold and shape embroideries to create fantastic freestanding sculptures.

Basic Dissolving

Dissolving can be done under a running tap or in a bucket of water, whichever you prefer. I personally work with a bucket of water so I can closely control how much water-soluble fabric is washed out.

Temperature plays a significant role in how quickly your fabric will dissolve. Water-soluble fabric dissolves slowly in cold water and as the water temperature increases, so will the speed of your dissolving. I always work with hot water because it is quick, and by using a consistent water temperature I have developed a good sense for when to remove the piece from the water to achieve my intended results. When working with hot water the water should feel hot to the touch, but never be so hot that it would burn you. Try experimenting with different water temperatures until you find the dissolving speed that suits you and your projects. Some people like to work quickly; some prefer to work slowly.

Method:

1. Before you dissolve a stitched drawing, trim off any excess water-soluble fabric from around the design. By doing this you help to keep the dissolving water clean and reduce the chances of getting a glue residue build-up on the final drawing. Your edge scraps can to be used for other smaller projects, so keep any decent sized pieces that will still fit into a hoop.

2. To dissolve the water-soluble fabric, submerge your embroidery in water and gently massage the embroidery with your fingers until the bulk of the fabric dissolves away. If you want to achieve some stiffening in the final product only submerge for a few seconds at most. The dissolving will happen very quickly: one second the fabric is there and the next it just seems to vanish. Alternatively, you can completely wash the water-soluble fabric out of the embroidery by agitating it thoroughly for several minutes in hot water or even soaking it overnight. This will leave you with a softer, more flexible end product which may suit your project better.

3. Once you have washed away the water-

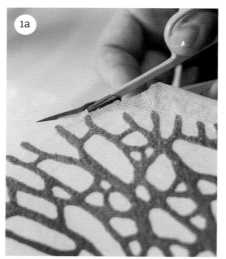

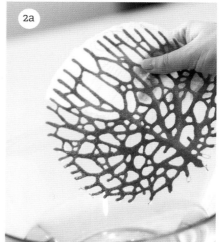

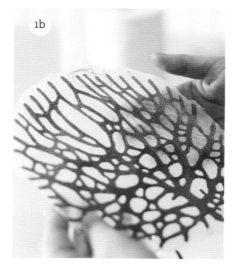

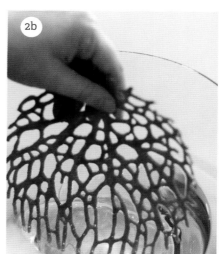

soluble fabric, lay the piece down on a bed of paper towels and absorb as much of the excess moisture as possible by blotting the embroidery with more paper towel. This is a very important step as it helps to remove any water-soluble fabric from the surface of the embroidery. If this residue is left on the surface it will dry as an undesirable white, glue-like substance over the surface of your embroidery.

4. Do not be tempted to leave your pieces to dry on paper towel—they will stick. Instead lay your piece to dry on a clean, smooth surface, such as a sheet of baking paper. Once the base fabric is removed your embroideries often take on a life of their own as they shrink and curl up in organic shapes and forms. This natural curling can result in some very interesting effects that you didn't initially predict. I often let my pieces crinkle and curl into whatever form they naturally take and this adds to the organic feel of the sculptures. However, if you want to flatten your embroidery as it dries, simply press the embroidery under something flat and heavy overnight. I find that large art books do the job nicely. Sandwich the embroidery between two sheets of baking paper to help keep the embroidery clean. When you remove your weights the next day your embroidery should be nice and flat. To prevent any warping, allow the piece to completely dry before moving it.

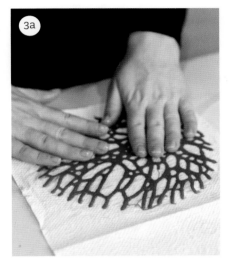

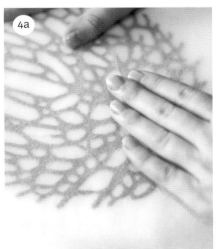

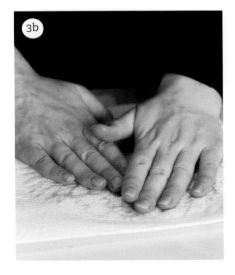

From flat to fabulous

Just because your embroidery is pressed flat doesn't mean it has to stay this way. There are many ways to transform a flat piece of embroidery into a dynamic artwork: you just need your imagination and a bit of planning.

Individual strips of embroidery can be twisted or folded back upon themselves for interesting effects. In this floral design every second strip of embroidery was twisted back to join up with another strip in the piece.

A spiral design will twist when it is hung from its central point creating an interesting three-dimensional form.

If you are planning to create an artwork that will twist, fold, or curl, it is a good idea to make a prototype of your design from paper first. This will help you refine the design before you start to stitch.

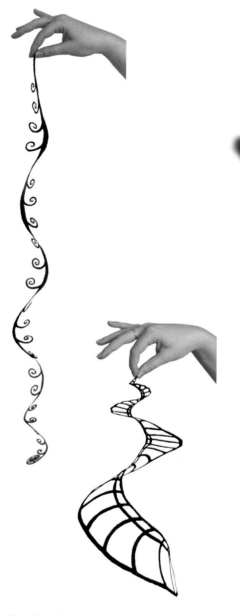

Floral Design, *2014, polyester thread and pins on paper, 16 x 16in (40 x 40cm)*

Spira mirabilis

The logarithmic spiral, often referred to as the "marvelous" spiral or by the Latin name *Spira mirabilis*, is found across the natural world. You will see this spiral curve in the chambers of a nautilus shell, in an unfurling fern frond, in the center of a sunflower, or in the swirling eye of a storm cloud. This spiral has a unique mathematical property in that as the size of the spiral increases, its shape is unaltered with each successive curve.

I am so often drawn to spiraling forms in my work and wanted to create an artwork that was inspired not by a particular plant or animal but by the simple concept of a spiral. So this artwork began with my studies into the *Spira mirabilis*, this unique mathematical spiral and the ways that it is repeatedly found in nature.

This piece was initially created and exhibited as a hanging artwork. After the exhibition I was playing with the piece in the studio and began to twist the individual fronds of the embroidery. This twisting curved the fronds back upon themselves and altered the overall form of the spiral, in the process adding a new dimension to the piece. I couldn't help but mount the piece with these new added twists, and the resulting artwork was *Spira mirabilis*.

Spira mirabilis, *2016, polyester thread and pins on paper, 36 x 41in (92 x 105cm).*

1. Spira mirabilis *presented as a hanging artwork.*
2. *Image of the final artwork (angled shot).*
3. Spira mirabilis *with the base fabric still intact, showing my original orientation and presentation of the fronds.*
4. *A detail of the final mounted* Spira mirabilis. *Note how the fronds now twist in the other direction.*

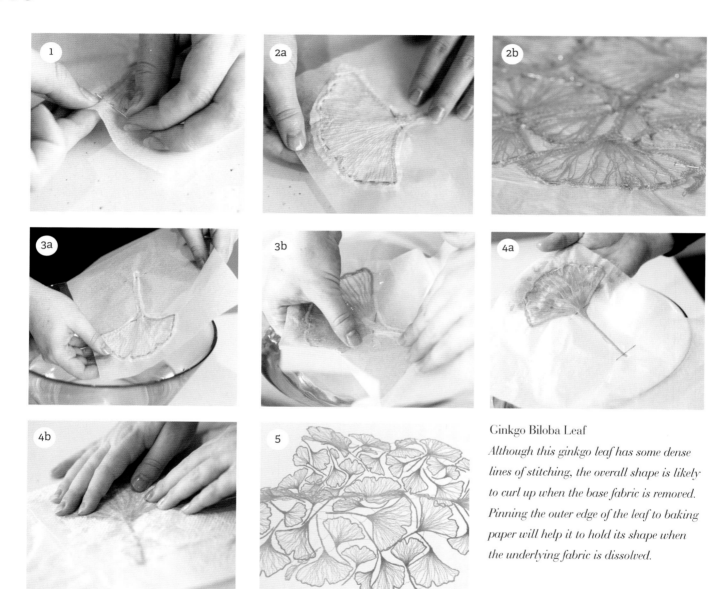

Ginkgo Biloba Leaf

Although this ginkgo leaf has some dense lines of stitching, the overall shape is likely to curl up when the base fabric is removed. Pinning the outer edge of the leaf to baking paper will help it to hold its shape when the underlying fabric is dissolved.

Supported Dissolving

A delicate stitched drawing may require some extra support to help it retain its shape when dissolving and drying. This extra support is especially important for single line drawings or designs that are likely to move, curl up, or distort when the base fabric is removed.

Method:

1. If a design needs some support to hold its shape while the base fabric is dissolved you can pin it to another surface prior to dissolving. I use baking paper as my supporting surface because it is affordable, readily available, and flexible. This latter quality is especially important when it comes to dissolving large pieces that may have to be folded to fit them into the dissolving bucket. Styrofoam sheets can be used as an alternative to baking paper but I find them to be bulky, fragile, and difficult to source.

2. I use stainless steel pins for dissolving because they will not rust after getting wet. When pinning embroidery to a support you are trying to secure the embroidery in a flat position. Start by laying the embroidery flat on a new sheet of baking paper. Weave a pin through the embroidery and the baking paper several times, as if you are stitching a line of running stitch with the pin. This will adhere the embroidery to the baking paper. It can be difficult to pin through very dense areas of embroidery. Instead try to weave the pin over any dense areas and hold the embroidery to the baking paper with a pin on either side. Keep pinning until you are confident that all areas that may curl or distort during dissolving are sufficiently secured. Make sure that all of your pins lie flush with the baking paper so there is less chance of getting stabbed by a pin: a painful hazard.

3. Submerge the embroidery and the baking paper into water to dissolve the base fabric. Gently massage the embroidery in the water for a few seconds in the same manner as an unsupported piece. The pins will help to hold the drawing in place and maintain the original shape of the stitched design.

4. Once the base layer has dissolved lay the embroidery and baking paper flat on your work surface. If a pin has shifted or fallen out during the dissolving process you can carefully weave it back into place. The water-soluble fabric can become trapped between the embroidery and the baking paper resulting in a glue-like residue on the final artwork. This can be avoided (or at least minimized) by absorbing as much of the excess water-soluble fabric as you can with paper towels.

5. Leave the embroidery attached to the support until the piece is completely dry.

Ginkgo Leaves

Kingdom: Plantae
Class: Ginkgoopsida
Order: Ginkgoales
Family: Ginkgoaceae
Genus: *Ginkgo*
Species: *G. biloba*

I saw my first ginkgo tree in the Royal Botanic Gardens in Sydney. I was lucky to visit the gardens while the tree was putting on its brilliant deciduous display. For a few weeks in fall the beautiful fan shaped leaves of the ginkgo turn a vivid buttery yellow and carpet the ground with color. I had never seen anything like it. The vision of this golden carpet has remained with me ever since.

The ginkgo is one of the oldest species on Earth and it has a fascinating history. This living fossil is a botanical oddity, being the only tree of its kind with no close living relatives. It is an ancient plant that has been virtually unchanged in 200 million years. The *Ginkgo biloba* also has a rich history of cultivation that has turned what was once a very rare Chinese tree into a common suburban occurrence worldwide.

These delicate, golden, fan shaped leaves have been the subject of many of my artworks over the last few years. I have created many life-sized versions of the leaves in various arrangements, as well as large-scale studies that map the unique vein pattern found within the foliage. I almost always depict the leaves in their iconic yellow color, even though they are only this shade for a short period of time each year.

Ginkgo biloba in Transition, *2014, polyester thread and pins on paper, 43 x 37in (109 x 95cm).*

Ginkgo Study #1, *2014, polyester thread and pins on paper, 20 x 24in (51 x 62cm).*

Molding and Sculpting

The glue-like nature of water-soluble fabric allows your stitched drawings to be molded into unique shapes. This opens up endless sculptural possibilities for your stitched drawings as you encourage them to twist, curve, and fold as they dry.

Molds

Almost anything can be used as a mold—you simply need a form that will support your embroidery and help it retain a consistent shape while it dries.

Solid objects make good molds provided you can drape or wrap the embroidery over or around them. The kitchen is always a good place to start to look for molds: ceramic and glass objects work well. If you want to hold your embroidery onto your solid mold you can wrap string or elastic bands around the embroidery to hold it in place while it dries.

Styrofoam is a great material for molds because it can be easily pinned into. This gives you extra control over how your embroidery sits while it dries. Additionally you can carve your own unique molds from blocks of Styrofoam, but this can be tricky and messy. Another option is to purchase pre-made Styrofoam shapes. The small, pre-made balls are my favorites because even the messiest piece of embroidery looks great once it is molded into a perfect sphere. I cover my Styrofoam shapes in aluminum foil before I use them. This helps to support the delicate surface of the foam from repeated pining, meaning I can reuse the molds again and again.

Simple molds made out of scrunched aluminum foil.

Further stiffening of sculptures

If you find that your sculptures need more stability once they are dry, you can further stiffen your embroideries with a fabric stiffener or glue. I find that a 50/50 mix of water and PVA glue applied in thin layers to the back of a piece can significantly stiffen a structure. However, this extra layer of glue can darken the thread colors or leave a shiny layer on the surface if used too freely. So always test your mix on a small sample piece first.

I am a big fan of using what is available and around you to help problem solve when you are creating. This is especially true when it comes to finding things to mold and shape your embroidered sculptures. This is a photo of some student work in progress from a workshop. Aside from the usual Styrofoam shape molds, these students created molds out of sticks from the local environment and even a bit of banana. Anything goes as far as molds are concerned!

Designing for Three Dimensions

When designing for three-dimensional projects you need to consider how your flat embroideries will behave once they are shaped around a mold. Embroideries may stretch, warp, or buckle when they are shaped, depending on the initial design and the shape they are molded onto. A bit of pre-planning and prototyping can help avoid unwanted warping or distortion in your embroidered forms.

Always design within the limits of your medium. Be realistic when you plan your sculptures—don't expect the water-soluble fabric to harden like steel and hold up huge areas of embroidery on its own. You are working with very soft, flexible materials and will have to take this into account when you design. If you want an embroidered sculpture to stand up on its own, try designing a sturdy structure that has many connection points or areas that overlap when you mold the embroidery.

Embroideries can be stretched, to a certain degree, when they are shaped—but how much stretch they can achieve depends upon on how densely the embroidery is stitched. Very loose, lace-like structures (such as a Scribble Sheet, see page 94) will have a fair bit of movement in them because they are a very mesh-like structure. These can be stretched over shallow curves to create seamless three-dimensional forms. More densely stitched embroideries will have less "give" and may buckle as they are shaped over curves. If you want to avoid this, the net shape of the design will need to include gaps that allow the embroidery to wrap around the mold without any buckling.

Paper prototypes are a good way to plan for three-dimensional embroideries. Getting the design correct in paper before you start to sew will help you predict and avoid possible issues or misalignments with your embroideries. This will save you time and possible heartache. To make a prototype simply draw the design on paper, then cut the design out imitating your vision for the final embroidery. You can then wrap the paper prototype around your mold in the same way you intend to shape the embroidery. If the prototype is not sitting happily, you can adjust it by cutting away areas, or adding more paper, until you are confident that the design will work as you intend. The paper prototype can then become a template for your embroidered design.

If you are unsure about a structure you have designed, give it a go anyway. Even if it fails you will learn from your mistakes and won't repeat them. Keep experimenting so you can discover, and perhaps push, the sculptural limits of this medium. You never know what wonderful things you may end up with.

Small circular scribble sheets have been molded over Styrofoam balls to form shallow, curved, cup shapes.

A growing twig bowl

This twig bowl is a fun little three-dimensional embroidery project. The design adapts to the specific needs of your mold as you work. This organic approach to sculptural embroidery means that you do not need a prototype, or strict mathematical plan, to build a strong structure. You just need to let it grow as you stitch.

This project hinges on the idea of creating a flat design that will eventually wrap around a mold to produce a smooth sculpture that connects at several points. These connections add strength to the structure, helping the sculpture to retain its molded form. In this instance I have used a basic line design, mimicking the way that new branches grow and fork, but you can experiment with whatever structures and patterns you like.

Method:

1. Draw a simple branching design on paper that radiates out from a central point. In this example I have drawn five branches that fork into smaller branchlets as they fan out, forming a rough circular shape. Make sure that none of the branches touch each other as this would form loops when the design is flat, resulting in pleating or buckling when the piece is on the mold.

2. Trace the design onto a piece of water-soluble fabric, then hoop the fabric ready for sewing.

3. Sew your design with your chosen stitching method. I have used the overlapping loops technique to build up dense lines of stitched branches.

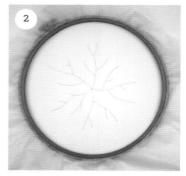

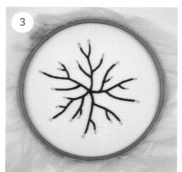

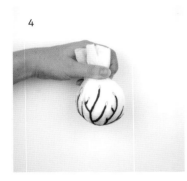

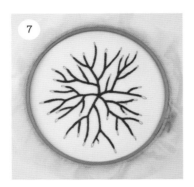

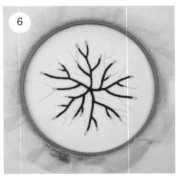

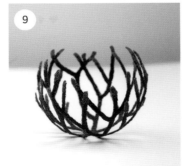

4. Remove your embroidery from the hoop and wrap it around your mold. In this instance I have used a Styrofoam ball, but you can use any type of mold you like.

5. Arrange the branches of the embroidery so that they are evenly splayed around the ball and sitting flat. Pinning the branches in place as you go may make this easier. By this stage you need the tips to connect—so check to see if there are points of contact where the branchlet tips connect or overlap the neighboring branch. Where there are areas that do not connect, extend your design by drawing directly onto the water soluble fabric so that these connections are made.

6. Remove the fabric from the mold and re-hoop the fabric ready for embroidery. Stitch the new areas that you have drawn.

7. Repeat steps 4–6 as many times as necessary until you are happy with the design and are confident that all of the branches will overlap at some point. Add any decorative elements that you like—I added some small green tips to the end of each of my branches. Dissolve your base fabric, then blot the excess water-soluble fabric and moisture away with paper towel.

8. Stretch the damp embroidery onto your mold, arranging the branches of your design in the desired position. Pin the branches into place and leave your sculpture to dry.

9. Once the sculpture is completely dry, gently remove it from the mold. If your branches come apart when you remove the mold you can reconnect them with a few hand stitches using the same color thread that you stitched your sculpture with.

Red Coral Bowl

The *Red Coral Bowl* is the largest molded embroidery I have made to date. This piece was created using the same approach as the twig bowl described before, just on a much larger scale. The design grew as I stitched: each time I put the piece back on the mold I would draw new lines mimicking the structures of gorgonian sea fans. When laid out flat, the design had many thin branches of embroidery that connected once it was put on the spherical mold. The circular shape in the center of the design acts as a base to help keep the form upright when it is displayed. This piece was stiffened with a watered down PVA solution to help the finished bowl retain its spherical shape.

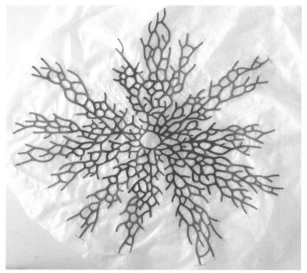

Final net shape of the Red Coral Bowl *before molding.*

Red Coral Bowl *in progress.*

Red Coral Bowl, *2016, polyester thread, 8in (20cm) diameter.*

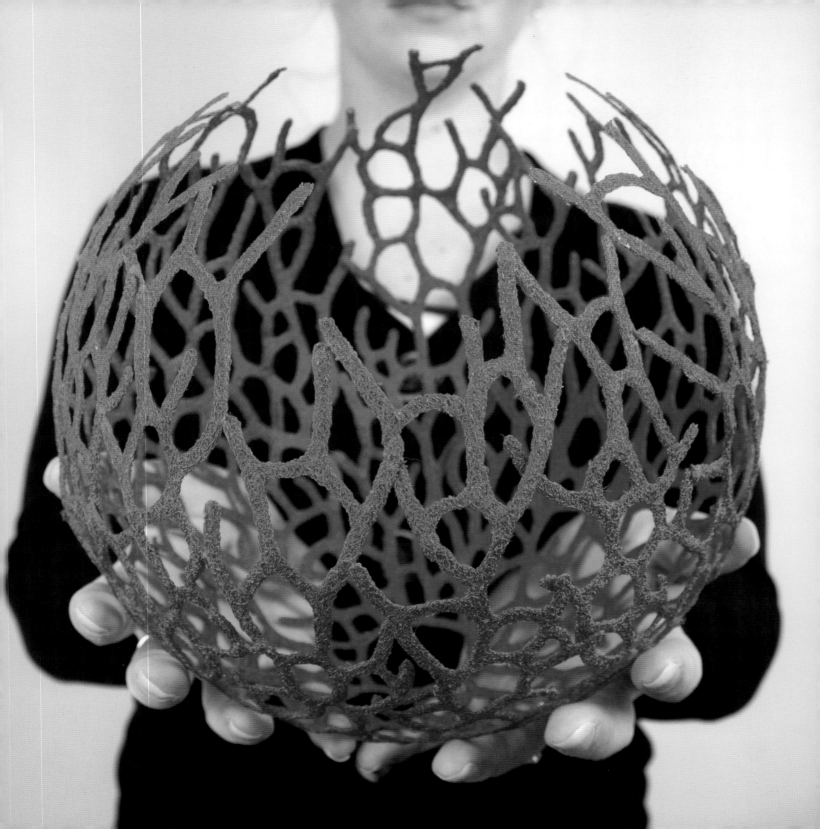

Tips and Troubleshooting

Tips, Tricks, and Trade Secrets

This chapter is the tips and tricks guide that I wish I'd had when I first started out with these techniques. It is the section of the book you can turn to when you have issues, or if you are completely new to machine embroidery and need a bit of help getting started. This chapter explores the more technical side of working with a sewing machine, detailing specific machine settings as well as machine care. This chapter also addresses ways to avoid and overcome some of the common issues you may encounter while stitching and dissolving your creations. By sharing some of my more technical tips, tricks, and trade secrets, I hope that you'll have great success with these embroidery processes.

Sewing Machine Setup Tips

Before you start any stitching project it is important to check that your sewing machine is in good working order and set up correctly. A sewing machine is a complex tool. The more informed you are about how your machine works and the correct way to use it, the more success and joy you will have when sewing.

Most sewing issues that I see in workshops are the result of user error. Students will be using either the wrong equipment for their specific machine, or using their machine incorrectly. Thankfully, most problems are easily rectified with a bit of education and the right equipment.

Bobbins

Check that your bobbin isn't bent or warped before you start sewing. Get rid of damaged bobbins so you won't accidentally use them.

Always use the correct bobbin for the make and model of your machine. Just because a bobbin fits into the bobbin case doesn't mean that it is the correct bobbin for that machine. There are cheap generic bobbins available on the market that will fit and work (to a certain degree) in most machines, but these bobbins can give you tension issues and will damage your machine over time. A good sewing supply store should be able to help you choose the correct bobbins for your make and model of machine.

Make sure that you have wound your bobbin correctly. A correctly wound bobbin should have the thread wrapped around it smoothly and tightly. If your bobbin is winding loose and loopy, check your manufacturer's instructions to confirm you are threading and winding the bobbin correctly.

Needles

Check that your needle is correctly installed and isn't blunt, burred, or bent before you start sewing. Make sure you are using the right needle for your thread. I work with "sharps" or "Jeans" needles (size 90) and they work well with the polyester machine embroidery thread that I use. A simple needle change is one of the quickest and easiest improvements you can make to your machine, so always have spare needles on hand.

Thread

Low quality threads will snap or shred when you attempt free-motion work. Always purchase good quality thread, even if it is a bit more expensive.

Check that your machine is correctly threaded. This sounds obvious, but incorrect threading is one of the commonest problems I see in workshops. Make sure you thread your machine with the presser foot raised, and that the thread is running freely and smoothly through your machine before you start sewing.

Horizontal threading vs. vertical threading

How you load your thread onto the machine can impact how smoothly your thread unravels and this in turn will affect your thread tension. Most machines have two thread pins, one with the option to load your thread vertically (spool standing up) and another to load the thread horizontally (spool lying down). Which loading option you choose will depend on the type of thread you are using and how it is wound onto the spool or cone.

A standard machine spool will have the thread wound around the spool in a single uninterrupted line and it is designed to wind off in the same way. Machine spools are best suited for use on your vertical pin so that the spool spins as the thread unwinds. If you were to put this type of spool on your horizontal pin you would be adding an extra twist to the thread every time a loop comes off the spool. This will make the thread thicker as it passes through your needle, contributing to thread shredding and breakage.

A cone of thread will have the thread wound on in a criss-cross pattern and this type of thread is designed to unravel from the top of the cone. Small cones of criss-cross wound threads will work well on your machine's horizontal pin. Larger cones will not fit on the horizontal pin and will require an external thread stand. A thread stand sits behind or off to the side of your machine and it will allow the cone to stand upright and the thread to unravel vertically and smoothly off the cone. I use large (3,000-meter) cones of thread so I always work with a thread stand.

Vertical thread stand with criss-cross wrapped cone of thread.

Above: Horizontal thread pin with criss-cross thread cone.   *Below: Vertical thread pin with a standard thread machine spool.*

Thread tension

Learning how to identify and correct tension issues is a basic, but very important, skill to have when it comes to understanding and operating a sewing machine. Both the top and the bottom (bobbin) tension settings work together to create consistent stitching. If your thread tension is correctly set, your stitches should look the same on both sides of your project.

To test your tension, machine draw some small circles or loops freehand and check if the thread is being dragged in on either side of the fabric. This dragging is often referred to as eyelashing. If the top side of your embroidery shows eyelashing the top thread tension is too tight and needs to be reduced (top thread tension numbers lowered). If there is eyelashing on the underside of your work the top thread tension is too loose and needs to be tightened (top thread tension numbers increased).

When setting your thread tension, always adjust your top thread tension first. Only ever adjust your bobbin tension if you find yourself at the limits of the top thread range and the tension is still not correct. Check your machine manufacturer's instructions for how to adjust your bobbin thread tension.

Top view.   *Underside (bobbin) view.*

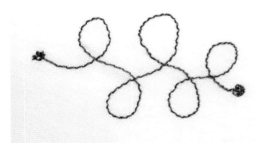
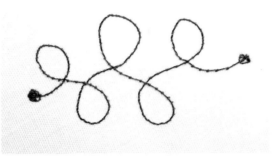

Correct thread tension
Stitches are even on both sides
of the fabric. No loops, pulls, or
"eyelashing" present.

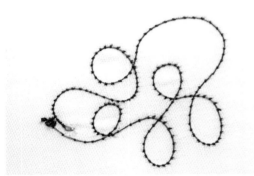
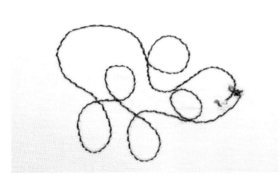

Tight top thread tension
The bobbin thread is being pulled
up to the top of the fabric and
creating slight eyelashing. The
top thread tension is too tight and
needs to be loosened.

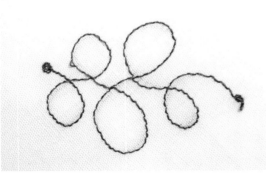
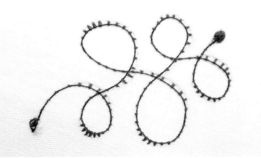

Loose top thread tension
The stitches are loose and looped.
The top thread is being dragged
to the underside of the fabric. The
top thread tension is too loose and
needs tightening.

Fine tuning thread tension for color blending

As you explore the thread tension setting on your machine you will probably discover that there is a range of top thread tension settings that provide the correct stitched surface. For example, you may find your stitches are even on both sides of the fabric when the top thread settings are anywhere between settings 2 and 4. This range allows you to fine tune the tension setting a little further to determine the optimal tension setting for color blending. Look for a setting that will achieve a stitched surface where both the top and bobbin threads are visible on one side of the embroidery, while still maintaining the correct tension for even stitching.

Choose two contrasting colors and thread your machine with one as the top thread and the other as the bobbin thread. In this example my top thread color is red and the bobbin thread color is blue. Stitch a dense section of embroidery to sample your color blend. I find the most effective way to do this is to stitch many overlapping loops, but feel free to experiment with the way you like to stitch. After stitching a patch of dense stitches examine the underside of your embroidery to see if both thread colors are visible. Adjust as necessary until you are happy with the blend.

Once you have determined the best tension setting for color blending, make a note of it and set your machine to this setting each time you do freehand machine embroidery. For example, I know that a setting of 2.75 is the best top thread tension setting for color blending on my machine. So I always set my machine to this setting when I do freehand machine embroidery. Keep in mind that different thread types and brands may have different thicknesses, so your color blend tension setting may need to change each time you use a different thread.

Top thread tension is too tight and only the bobbin color is visible. Reduce the top thread tension and try again.

Correct thread tension will result in dots of the top thread color coming through to the underside.

Top thread tension is too loose and it is affecting the stitch quality. The top thread is being dragged down to the underside of the embroidery making your embroidery very thick and loopy.

Note: All these images show the underside of the embroidery.

Hydrangea Petal, *2015,*
polyester thread and pins on
paper, 37 x 32in (93 x 82cm).

Machine Maintenance

As you explore this kind of embroidery you will probably clock some solid hours at your sewing machine. To keep your machine working at optimum level, basic maintenance—such as regular cleaning and oiling—is necessary. You should aim to clean and oil your machine for every eight to ten hours of sewing you do.

Cleaning your machine

A sewing machine needs to be regularly cleaned and oiled to optimize its function and ensure that the machine parts are not wearing out prematurely. This maintenance is quick and easy to perform and it will help your machine run quietly and stitch smoothly.

To clean your machine, first turn it off and unplug it from the power source. Remove the bobbin case and throat plate. Using a stiff-bristled lint brush, sweep out any threads or lint that have built up around the feed dogs and in the bobbin compartment. If you have a front-loading bobbin, remove the shuttle hook and brush out any lint and threads from this area. Avoid using compressed air or your own breath to blow dust out of your machine. Both of these can blow the lint further into the mechanisms and will introduce moisture to the machine, which can cause corrosion.

Oiling your machine

Oiling is slightly different for every make and model of machine so it is important to check your manufacturer's instructions to ensure you are oiling your machine correctly. Follow the instructions in your machine manual carefully; don't be tempted to just oil every moving part as this is unnecessary and will make a huge mess. Do not use car oil or any other oil that is not specifically sewing-machine oil. Most machines will be sold with a small vial of oil that is suited to that particular make and model of machine.

Only use a small amount of oil. One drop is usually enough. Over-oiling a machine will result in a very messy bobbin compartment and the oil will leach up onto your work as you stitch. After oiling it is a good idea to run some scrap fabric through your machine a few times with a basic straight stitch to pick up any excess oil that may be drawn up and out of the machine.

If your machine manual tells you not to oil the machine it is likely that you have a self-lubricating machine that does not require oiling by the user. Do not be tempted to oil your machine if your manual tells you not to. A self-lubricating machine will still need oil and maintenance from a machine mechanic, so regular servicing is very important for these machines.

Servicing your machine

Even if you are cleaning and oiling your machine on a regular basis you are only maintaining a small part of a very complicated system. The rest of your machine will need further oiling and maintenance and this should be left to a trained sewing machine mechanic. It is suggested that you service your machine annually, or every 100 hours of stitching. Don't wait until something goes wrong with your machine to take it in for service. Regular servicing and care will ensure that you will enjoy your machine for many years.

Brushing lint and threads out from underneath the throat plate.

Some machines will have clearly marked ports for you to oil during home maintenance. These are usually marked in red.

Oiling the shuttle. If you have a front-loading bobbin you will need to remove the shuttle hook for oiling. The outer edge of the shuttle will require only one small drop of oil.

Drawing on water-soluble fabric

If you are drawing a very complex or large artwork design you may want to trace some guidelines to follow. Water-soluble fabric is very easy to trace designs onto as it is somewhat transparent. Ideally you want a pen or marker that you can follow when stitching but that will not be visible on the final artwork after the base fabric is dissolved. I have experimented with many markers, pens, pencils, and chalks and I have yet to find the perfect product for all my projects. However, I do have some suggestions for what to use and what not to use, in specific situations.

Whenever you draw on your water-soluble fabric you want to put the least amount of marks on the fabric as possible. The less ink on the fabric, the less chance there is of color from the markers leaching through and contaminating the final artwork.

Don't use:

- **Lead pencil**—This will muddy up your work and make it look dirty.
- **Water-based markers**—These reactivate in water and can leach through your work when the base fabric is dissolved. They can also weaken or put holes in your base fabric if you use them too heavily.

Try using:

- **Fine line, permanent markers** Because these are alcohol based they do not affect the stability of your water-soluble fabric and will not reactivate and bleed when they get wet. However, the color from these markers will still be trapped within your drawing when you dissolve it, so always use a marker color that is similar to the threads.

- **Heat-erasable "Frixion" pens** These pens are made up of a combination of gel and thermo ink and if you blast your piece with a hot hairdryer prior to dissolving, their color will fade away. Keep in mind that these pens were not designed for use on fabric and if the artwork gets very cold the color may reappear.

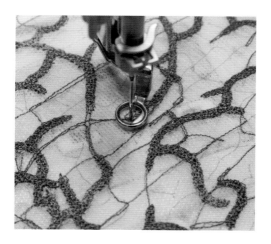

Working with light or white threads

When I work with white threads I often stitch the entire design freehand to avoid any risk of color contamination from a drawn guideline. This is a very organic way to embroider because the design can grow and evolve as you stitch. Working freehand, with no drawn guidelines, can be challenging if you want to create large or detailed designs. If you want to work with white or light colored threads and you feel you must follow a drawn guideline I have a few suggestions:

- Always put the least amount of pen possible onto your water soluble fabric. Draw your guidelines with light dots rather than solid lines.
- Avoid putting any marks directly where you plan to stitch. Instead draw your guidelines slightly off to the side of your planned stitch line. I find that by lining my drawn guideline up with the edge of my machine foot (rather than the needle) I will stitch a few millimeters away from my guideline. This gives me a slight buffer between the drawn line and my embroidery and helps ensure that my stitching doesn't touch the pen ink.
- Trim away the drawn guidelines before you dissolve the base fabric to ensure that there is no ink on the fabric. This can be tedious work but it is worth it to ensure a clean, mark free final embroidery.

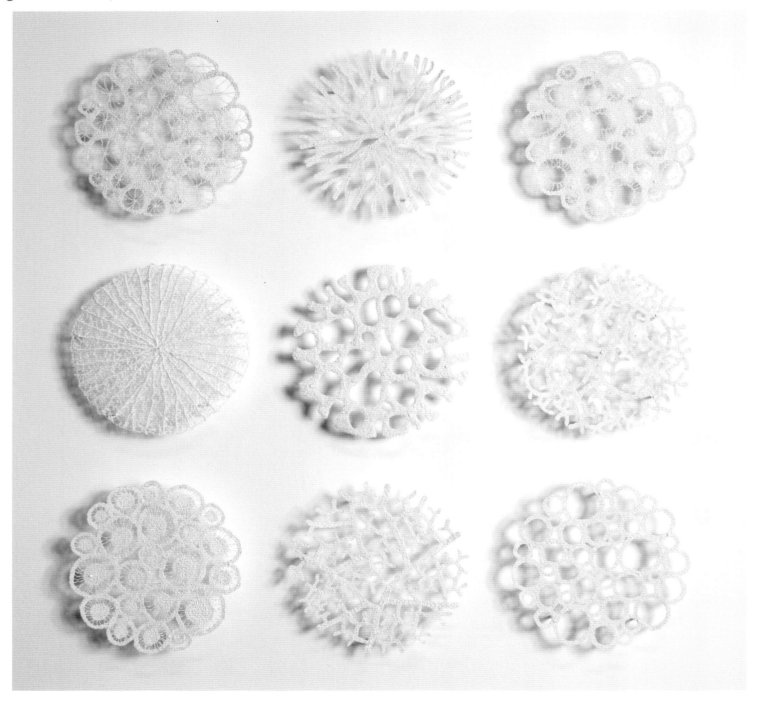

***Stitched Specimens* in white**

Each of the pieces that made up this collection of stitched specimens was embroidered without any guidelines or markings on the base fabric. They were drawn completely freehand and the design evolved as I was stitching. Each of these stitched specimens is inspired by a natural structure that grows and divides: some are based on branching leaf veins or corallite clusters, others mimic cellular structures.

Stitched Specimens, *2015, polyester thread and pins on paper, 27 x 27in (70 x 70cm).*

Stitching Tips

Allowing for shrinkage: Your embroidery will shrink a little when you wash away the base fabric because you are removing that supportive material. The amount of shrinkage will depend entirely upon how densely you stitch your designs. Very densely stitched pieces where the stitches are very close together will have only a small amount of shrinkage, while looser designs where the stitches are farther apart will shrink more. I find that my dense stitching style results in shrinkage of between five and ten percent. It is good practice to plan for this inevitable shrinkage when you are designing an artwork, especially if you need your final stitched drawings to be a specific size.

Stitch at a consistent speed: When you sew at a consistent speed you will get into a good rhythm and your embroidered drawings will look more uniform as a result. A consistent speed will also put less strain on your machine and threads, resulting in fewer thread breakages and machine snags. In my experience, if things are going to go wrong while you are stitching, it usually happens when you are starting, stopping, or changing speeds. "Smooth and steady" is a good mantra to stitch by. When I work I run my machine as fast as it will go the whole time, so that my stitching speed is always the same (around 1,000 stitches per minute).

Fast feet but slow hands: Work up to running the machine at a consistently fast speed while moving your hoop in a slow controlled manner. Don't feel that you need to "keep up" with the machine like you would if the feed teeth were up. Aim for stitches that are close together so that you make lots of connection points in your work; this will help to create tighter and neater embroidered drawings.

Check your connections: This type of embroidery is all about your connection points. If your drawing isn't well connected it will fall apart once you wash away the base fabric—which can be heartbreaking. It is very important to ensure that all of your stitched lines connect precisely where you want them. To avoid any problem, give your work a good final check over before you dissolve the backing fabric.

Looking to the light: Get into the habit of periodically holding your stitched drawings up to a light source so that they are backlit. This will help you to identify areas where your stitched lines aren't quite connected, so you can go back and fix up the parts you have missed. "Looking to the light" is also a good way to check your stitch density. I am very conscious about keeping my stitch density consistent across the project, so that any shrinkage is even across the piece. Your drawing doesn't need to be so densely stitched that no light can penetrate the stitches. As long as the design is completely connected and you are happy with how the piece looks and feels, you are ready to dissolve your drawing.

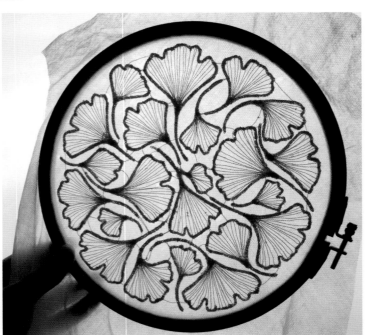

Avoiding holes and tears

Water-soluble fabric will tear easily if it is not treated with great care. Holes in your embroideries may distort your design, plus they are very frustrating, so they are best avoided. There are several practices that will help to avoid holes in your fabric:

- Don't stretch your water-soluble fabric too tightly. Extremely tightly stretched fabric is more likely to tear under the strain when you start stitching. Your fabric should be stretched so that it is flat and tight (like a drum), but not so tight that it is under stress.
- You may notice that water-soluble fabric is softer and weaker on very hot, humid days. As a precaution I wear a pair of cotton gloves on very hot days so that the heat and moisture in my hands does not weaken the fabric when I am sewing.

Support stitching

Holes most commonly occur when there is a change in sewing direction (typically at a corner or sharp turn), or at the ends of lines of dense stitching. If I know that there is a part of my design that may be vulnerable to tears I will stitch a loop or bolstering line of preventative support stitches. These stitches are not a part of the artwork design, but are there simply to help ensure my fabric stays intact while I sew. Support stitches can be removed from the final artwork by trimming the threads off with sharp embroidery scissors: you will never know they were there.

The tips of these leaves are vulnerable to fabric tears because there are many stitches pulling on one small part of the fabric. To help prevent holes I stitched small loops at the tip of each leaf and never had any problem with tearing. Once the piece was dissolved and dry these loops were trimmed off with sharp embroidery scissors.

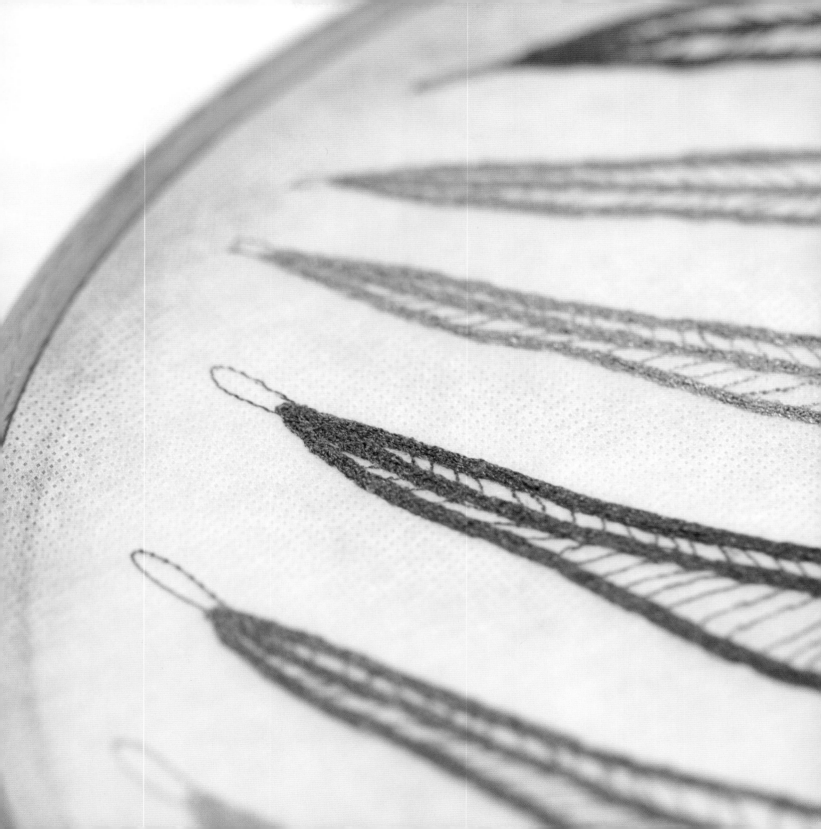

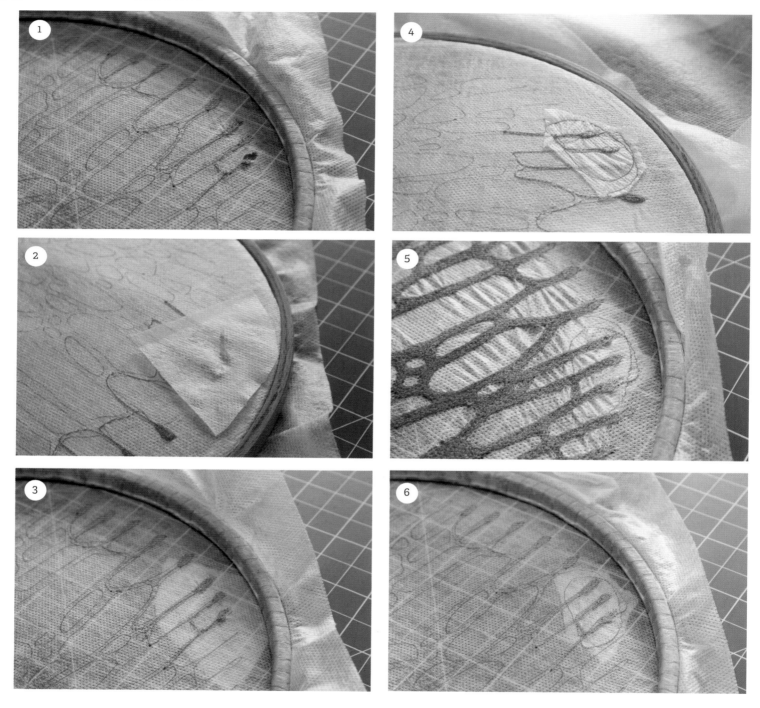

Patching holes

Sometimes, despite your best efforts, holes happen. Small holes in your work are not the end of the world, or your embroidery. Holes can be patched with small pieces of water-soluble fabric placed behind the hole and tacked in place with a few support stitches. Always try to catch holes while they are still small, preferably under a quarter of an inch (1cm) across. Very large holes or tears in the fabric can dramatically affect the tension of your fabric in the hoop and cause your design to distort when you stitch.

Method:

1. A small hole in your embroidery can be easily repaired with a patch of scrap water-soluble fabric.
2. The patch should be large enough to cover the hole and at least half an inch (1-2cm) on either side of the hole.
3. Position the patch on the underside of the embroidery to avoid it getting caught in your presser foot.
4. Stitch the patch in place with single lines of stitching before you attempt to stitch over the hole.
5. The stitch lines that were used to anchor the patch in place can be removed after the piece is dissolved.
6. The patch can be stitched over many times to complete your design.
7. Completed repair.

Dissolving Tips

More support stitches

One of the best ways to avoid issues when dissolving is to pre-plan for these issues when you are stitching your design. If you anticipate that a design may curl up or distort when you wash away the base fabric, you can lay down some temporary supporting stitches to hold the design in place when it is washed. This is also helpful if you have a design made up of many individual pieces that you want to keep connected when you dissolve the base fabric. These lines of support stitches will help hold your design together when it is being dissolved and may prevent the design curling up or distorting. These support stitches can be removed later.

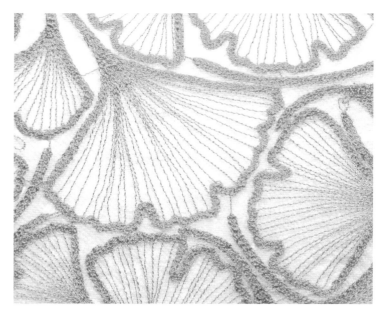

This design is made up of many individual ginkgo leaves. I purposefully connected the leaves with single lines of stitching when I was sewing the design. This helps to keep the piece together while it is being dissolved and mounted. Having served their purpose, these connecting lines were removed after the piece was mounted.

The two pieces of the Fan Worm Crown *were made up of many radiating lines. Because these lines are not connected anywhere except the center of the design they have the potential to curl up and distort once the base fabric is removed. To help prevent this, I laid down a circle of support* *stitches around the outer edges of the piece. This helped to stabilize my stitching and prevent holes. This stitching also helped to keep the piece flat as it was dissolved. These support stitches were carefully cut away once the piece was dissolved and completely dry.*

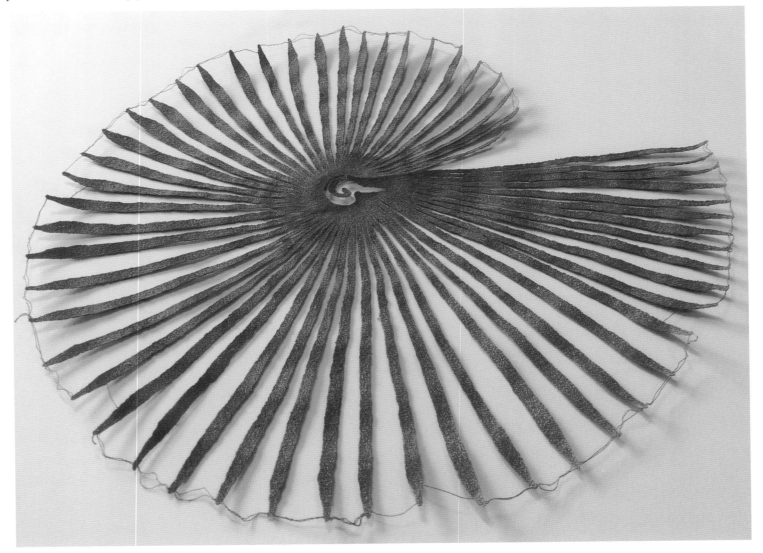

Glue residue on fabric

Excess water-soluble fabric will show up as a whitish residue on your embroideries when they are dry. This gluey crust can be very frustrating when you have spent so long on an embroidery and it looks like a snail has come along and left a slime trail all over it. When the water-soluble fabric is wet it turns clear so it can be difficult to see where these glue residue areas are lurking. So, look closely at your dissolved pieces to see if any thick, clear, paste-like areas remain on the embroidery—this is the excess water-soluble fabric. Dab off this excess paste with paper towel while the piece is still wet and you are less likely to have residue on the finished, dry piece.

If you end up with residue on a piece, you can often gently scrape it off with your fingernail, or gently trim it off with embroidery scissors. If you have a piece that has a lot of residue present it is possible to rewet the piece, even if it has dried.

Rewetting your pieces after they have dried

If you are not happy with the shape your embroidery has dried in or your piece has excessive residue that you cannot scrape or cut off, it is possible to wet the piece again. Simply follow the same dissolving processes I outlined earlier. Keep in mind that rewetting your artwork will wash more of the water-soluble fabric out of your embroidery resulting in a softer and more flexible piece.

Trimming messy threads from a finished piece of embroidery

After you have dissolved your embroidery you may discover lines of stitching that are in places you don't want them. Or you may have added support stitches to your embroidery that you now want to remove. These threads are easily removed by trimming them off with your embroidery scissors. Because the water-soluble fabric has glued the thread fibers together they should trim off with a neat edge and not fray. Make sure you only trim these threads off when your embroidery is completely dry.

Quick Troubleshooting Guide

My stitches are loose and messy: Your tension setting may need adjusting, or you may be stitching without the presser foot lowered. If you haven't lowered your presser foot you will have no top thread tension and this results in very messy loose threads on the underside of the drawing.

Top thread snapping: Lower your top thread tension. Rethread your machine after every break. If the thread still keeps breaking, try using a different thread.

Top thread shredding: Change to a fresh needle. Reduce top thread tension slightly. Rethread the machine. If the thread keeps shredding, try using a different thread.

Needle keeps breaking: Make sure that your needle and throat plate are correctly installed. Needle breakages often happen when you move the embroidery hoop too quickly and the needle bends and hits the throat plate. To help avoid this move your hoop at a slow, consistent speed.

Tearing holes in water-soluble fabric: Make sure that your feed dogs are turned off. Avoid sharp changes of direction when you are stitching. If you tear small holes in your fabric you can patch the hole with a small piece of base fabric placed behind your stitching (see page 171 for more details).

Thread knotting underneath: If you get a tangle of threads under your stitching it is likely that the top thread has slipped off the take up arm at some point. Rethread your top thread.

Thread jamming underneath: This is often called a thread lock and it can be caused by an incorrectly threaded bobbin, dust or lint around the bobbin compartment, or incorrect tension. Remove the embroidery from machine. Take out the bobbin case and shuttle and remove any tangled thread in the bobbin case compartment. Check that the compartment is clean of dust and lint. Rethread the machine.

Machine making horrible noises / not moving / doing strange things, etc.: If no matter what you try or how many times you clean, oil, or rethread your machine it just won't behave, there may be something out of alignment, broken, or jammed in your machine. If this is the case take it to a professional sewing machine mechanic for service and repair.

References and Acknowledgments

This book has been a huge undertaking and there are many people who helped along the way. I would like to thank:

Schiffer Publishing and Blue Red Press, for taking this project on and making this dream a reality. Especially Jo for guiding this very naive artist through the wonderful world of book making.

Gez, for taking all of the photos that I couldn't take myself. You did a great job of hiding my huge baby bump. Sorry that I chose one of the hottest days of the year to do fieldwork.

The many wonderful friends and family who read my drafts or let me use them as a sounding board as I pulled this book together. Your encouragement and keen editing skills made all the difference.

David, my amazing husband. For your many years of support and logistical engineering. None of what I do is possible without you.

Finally to Charlotte, my daughter. This book is dedicated to you.
You won't remember it, but you were with me throughout the entire creation of this book (both in and out of the belly). So many people thought I was crazy for writing a book with a newborn. They were probably right. But you made the crazy a lot of fun.